ADVANCE PRAISE

"The study abroad field has needed this kind of book for a long time. It's written for students in a way that's the perfect mix of supportive, insightful, and instructive with a lively wit that encourages them to squeeze every moment out of their precious experience. Kurtzman's decades of experience in the field shows, but it's his sincerity of purpose and desire to guide every student toward maximizing their journey that really makes the difference. Don't let your students study abroad without it!"

—Melissa Torres,
President and CEO of the Forum on Education Abroad

"*Like a Fish in Water* is the one and only resource I recommend to all students who are considering study abroad. This book is a must-read for students and families as they prepare for one of their most important and enriching educational journeys. It provides reassurance, critical advice, and guidance that I haven't seen in any other writing."

—Devika Milner,
Assistant Dean and Director of Study Abroad
at the University of Miami

"The activities in this book were so helpful to me before, during, and after studying abroad. *Like a Fish in Water* explains everything clearly and in a fun way. This book helped me feel incredibly supported and would help anyone who might feel nervous about getting the most out of the experience."

—Brenley Bruxvoort,
study abroad student

"I wish this book had been around when my oldest son studied abroad. The journey can be really challenging, and this book is like a warm, caring mentor who will tell it like it is, offer some laughs along the way, and provide just the right advice and tools to embrace the ride and grow through it. I'm so grateful my younger son will have its benefits when he studies abroad!"

—Carla Slawson,
Executive Director of the Arthur J. Schmitt Foundation

LIKE A FISH IN WATER

LIKE A FISH IN WATER

How to Grow Abroad When You Go Abroad

RICH KURTZMAN

LIONCREST
PUBLISHING

*To all of the students who take the leap into new cultural waters
and to all who support them.*

CONTENTS

FOREWORD

—Troy Peden,
Founder of GoAbroad.com

*Study abroad is perhaps the most transformational
educational experience students can have.*

Study abroad has been waiting for a book like this, and I can't think
of anyone who is better suited to write it. Rich Kurtzman is a widely
respected thought leader in International Education—frequently speaking
around the world, teaching students abroad, preparing them before they
depart, leading programs in Europe, and working directly with thousands
of students as their perspectives are broadened and their lives are changed.
Rich doesn't just get international education from a theoretical perspective;
he has lived and breathed it, alongside students, for over two decades.

Rich has devoted his career to helping students maximize the outcomes
of their international experience and to training the trainers—teaching
international educators tips and strategies to increase cultural awareness.
Rich is passionate about cultivating learning across cultures.

Many students report their study abroad experience as the most important thing they did at university, but very few will say it was without
challenges, hurdles, and hiccups. This book will help transform those
bumps into opportunities. It's like having a cultural mentor alongside
you for the entire journey!

Like a Fish in Water is essential reading for any student (as well as their parents) before they go abroad, while they are on their program, and even after they return home. The stories will entertain you, the activities will guide you, and the outcomes will inspire you.

The world needs more students like you who will come away with a broader perspective, a deeper understanding of themselves, and an empathy for other cultures. You'll gain confidence, resilience, and adaptability, and you'll do it while having the time of your life. My sincerest congratulations to you on your decision to take this leap.

INTRODUCTION

I was living the dream. Literally, living *my* dream. I was living and working in the cosmopolitan capital of the Mediterranean, Barcelona! From the terrace of my apartment, every morning I could have my café con leche while looking out over one of the greatest cities in the world—from views of the sea, to Gaudi's famous Sagrada Familia church, to Tibidabo, the highest peak of Barcelona. I should have been on top of the world.

So, why, after only four months, did I want to wake up from this dream come true? Why did I feel more depressed than I ever had in my life? Why did I want to leave it all behind and move back home to Chicago?

When I was in college, as a study abroad student in Madrid, I fell in love with Spain, and I dreamed of moving there one day. I had to. I loved the culture, the people, the food, the language, the challenges, and the opportunities. Fast forward to four years later, to the moment they told me I got the job in Barcelona, and I jumped up and bear-hugged the HR manager.

But then, after a couple of months abroad, many of those aspects of Spanish culture that I had loved turned into things that I hated. Stores being closed on Sundays frustrated me for the lack of convenience. I was sick of the same food and just wanted my comfort foods from back home. I didn't quite "get" the locals, and they didn't quite "get" me—it seemed that our values weren't in line. Because of the cultural differences, I didn't feel like I fit in, and it was an awful feeling. I found myself repeatedly thinking, *Why did I do this to myself? Why didn't I just stay home?*

The funny thing is I had these same thoughts when I studied abroad in St. Petersburg, Russia, then again when I studied in Madrid, and again during my internship in Milan, Italy.

Why did I want to put myself through those challenges overseas? Why struggle through the discomfort, loneliness, mishaps, and cultural blunders?

The answer was clear: deep down, I knew that all of those study and intern experiences would be life-changing. They were some of my best investments in time, energy, and money, for so many reasons, reasons that I'll make clear in this book. Still, at that moment, I was ready to quit.

That's when "The Future Me Letter" saved the day. When I was ready to throw it all in, say, "screw this," and move back, I called my mom to tell her I was giving up and coming home. She said, "That's not happening," and reread The Future Me Letter I had written to her right before I left. I had given it to her at the airport as we said goodbye with tears flowing down our cheeks. The letter read: "At some point, I am going to tell you this is too hard, and I'm going to want to come home... DON'T LET ME!"

Enduring the ups and downs of those study abroad experiences, in college, gave me exactly what I needed to get through the biggest challenge I would face. And "previous me" knew that. "Previous me" also knew that, when I eventually worked through those dark days and challenges, I would turn them into the best experiences of my life.

WILL YOU FEEL THE MAGIC?

You've seen it before—a friend comes back from study abroad, and they are beaming. They had the experience of a lifetime. They've had a transformation.

All study abroad programs and study abroad offices tell you that it will change your life.

And it's true. I've seen it happen. It absolutely happened to me, and I've been alongside thousands of students who have felt the study abroad "magic." They grew more confident, resilient, adaptable, self-aware, and worldly. They landed their dream job because of their study abroad experience. They no longer stress about the little things and are willing to take on anything the world throws at them, because they've conquered bigger issues in other countries, cultures, and languages.

But in my twenty-five years working in International Education, I've also seen too many students who wasted the opportunity. Some couldn't handle the challenges and left early. Others strolled through their time abroad leisurely and skimmed across the surface but didn't transform in the ways that so many others have.

The difference between that first group of students and the second is that those who felt the magic had the right tools to guide them. They knew what they had to do to maximize the experience. They also understood that a life-changing experience abroad includes bumps along the way. That's part of what this book is about: discover the magic, but don't expect perfection.

I want to help you along this journey. I want to take everything I've learned and make sure you don't miss out. This has been my passion and mission for the majority of my life.

TRANSFORMATION

The students I've worked with who have had the proper guidance while abroad leave transformed. Here is what two of them had to say:

"It can be so difficult to put into words how much my experience has impacted me, as I've learned so much about myself through studying abroad. I realized that by getting to know the people and the culture of the place you're visiting, it changes how you experience it. It can be easy to visit and be the typical tourist; however, since I've been able to get to know the people and culture of

this city, it's allowed me to break down that tourist wall and really experience the authentic life here. Wherever I travel in the future, my experience abroad has shown me how to do that."
—Brianna F.

"The most valuable thing that I learned abroad is to not be afraid to do things I've never done before. My main goal studying abroad was to push myself outside my comfort zone. It was difficult at first, but I definitely learned a lot about myself and grew as a person by trying out so many new things!"
—Bryan K.

Deciding to study abroad could be the best decision you've ever made. You can have the time of your life and gain essential skills that lead to a happier and healthier future, while also helping you land your dream job. What else could you possibly do that offers the same?!

WHAT THIS BOOK CAN DO FOR YOU

The magic of study abroad will be a myth to you if you don't approach it with the right mindset and tools. The experience is like most things in life: you get out of it what you put into it.

But how do you know what to put into it? I don't want you to leave it up to chance! Just studying abroad doesn't guarantee that you will see this transformation in yourself. It takes work. You need to actively participate in the experience.

→ Activities in the Book

Throughout the book, I will be suggesting activities I've developed or borrowed that will guide you throughout your time abroad. When I teach, I give these activities as homework, and my students actually thank me—for giving them homework! That's because these exercises lead to the "aha moments" that are so impactful.

I've labeled the activities "ACT" instead of "Activities" because this is not a passive venture you are embarking on; it's a very active one.

I've chosen one activity per chapter, labeled "Fast Track," which I would suggest you do if you feel you can only do one (although I hope you do them all!).

Also, at the end of every chapter, there is a section called "Dive Deeper Into…"—a brief list of resources you can use if your interest is piqued and you want to learn more about any of the content in the chapter.

By reading this book and following the activities, you'll experience the journey in a richer and more meaningful way. This book will coach you, step-by-step, activity-by-activity, through the entire experience, from before you even leave until long after you return, when you are sitting in that job interview, talking about all that you learned during study abroad.

Don't worry about reading it all in one sitting. In fact, it's better if you don't. This book will accompany your journey as you experience it, which doesn't happen overnight; nor should it.

→ Some Notes to Keep in Mind While Reading This Book:

- I am a big believer in the power of both interning and studying abroad. To simplify, I just say "study abroad" throughout the book, but if you are interning abroad, you can easily substitute "intern abroad" in almost all instances.

- I am acutely aware that my cultural lens (which you will learn is VERY important) is of a White, middle-class male from the suburbs of Chicago who is very interested in education and learning.

Everyone reading this book will come to it from a different cultural lens. I've tried to take that into account throughout.

- This book is geared towards students at US colleges and universities leaving the US to study in another country. I recognize and appreciate that many of those students will also come from multicultural backgrounds and, so, will have unique cultural lenses. Some of you may be studying abroad, in the US, and are now embarking on another study abroad journey. That's brilliant!

- When using the words "America" or "American," I am referring to the United States, and not all of North America or Central or South America. I use this for ease of reference and because, linguistically, this is a common usage. I mean no offense to anyone from another part of the Americas.

WHAT'S NOT IN THIS BOOK

This book is not about packing lists, electrical converters, or vaccine and visa requirements. There are plenty of places you can go to find those logistics. This book goes much deeper than all of that. There's one exception: I do give suggestions for packing from a cultural perspective, in Chapter 10. Skip ahead if that's one of your burning questions right now.

Full books could and should be written about health and safety and risk-management protocols for study abroad. This is not that book. I recommend you talk to your study abroad office and program provider about the precautions they can provide.

Nor does this book give you all of the answers. It doesn't tell you that, in England, you must do this or, in Italy, you can expect that for every situation. But it does give you the tools to find out that important information for yourself, and that's part of your journey.

WHAT IS IN THIS BOOK

This book is your toolbox filled with the things you never knew you needed.

This book is ideal for a student at any stage of the process, whether you're not getting on that airplane for months or you're already abroad. Even if you're already home from your experience, this book will walk you back through your time abroad, to see it from a different perspective and reveal ways in which you may have grown.

I still use these tools myself whenever I travel. They enabled me to take Muay Thai lessons in Thailand with a professional fighter; to explore a sensory-filled food market in Oaxaca, Mexico, with a local who then taught me to make the best enchiladas de mole; and to create lasting friendships in Barcelona.

Whether you're studying on a short program, a semester, or a year, this book is for you. The duration doesn't matter; it's your engagement that counts.

You'll learn about the proper mindset, how to overcome the challenges, how to laugh at your mistakes and learn from them, how to connect with people from all over the world, and then how to put all of that together to help make you more employable.

Think of it this way: you could walk through the Louvre Museum in Paris and admire the *Mona Lisa*, but if you have a guide who explains Leonardo da Vinci's brushstrokes, the use of light and shadow, the history of that era, and how to compare this work to other masterpieces, you will walk away enlightened. I want to use my experience to help enlighten you about the magic of study abroad. I want you to experience that magic—in ways you can't even imagine right now—instead of just coming home saying, "It was great!"

Together we'll discover the beauty of making:

- The unfamiliar, familiar
- The unusual, usual
- The unpredictable, predictable
- The unimaginable, imaginable

ORIGIN OF THE BOOK

International education has been my whole professional career. Working with students to help them see the world from a different perspective, create lightbulb moments, and learn to grow when they go abroad has been my number one professional goal. It's why I started my study abroad program, it's why I teach culture classes and work as an intercultural consultant, and it's especially why I still travel the world and put all of this into practice myself—no matter where I go—so I can keep learning about other cultures and push myself out of my comfort zone.

MY JOURNEY AND WHAT IT MEANS TO YOUR JOURNEY

Successfully living in other cultures is my everyday experience. My wonderful wife is from England, and our two young kids are trilingual (English, Spanish, Catalan) and quad-cultural (British, American, Spanish, and Catalan).

Despite wanting to give it all up after four months, I'm still loving life in Barcelona, twenty years later.

I am originally from just outside Chicago, and I never left the US until I was twenty years old. My first experience requiring a passport was when I studied in St. Petersburg, Russia, where I lived with a homestay family and took classes on a local campus. I was WAY out of my comfort zone. I made a million mistakes. I got lost. I got myself in trouble. I had to take showers by boiling water, mixing it with colder water, and using a bucket.

And I loved it! I wouldn't change a minute of it.

I made friends with people from around the world. I felt comfortable in a home away from home. I improved my language skills immensely. The uncomfortable started to feel comfortable. The unknown started to feel known. The unpredictable started to feel predictable. My view of the world developed. My view of the US evolved. I learned more about myself than I ever thought I could.

That led me to do it again. I studied in Madrid, Spain, for a semester, and went through the same ups and downs; I loved it so much that I knew I wanted to work in this field of study abroad, to help other students experience the same highs, lows, and growth as I did.

So I started working with a study abroad company in Chicago; I took summers off to lead high-school students in Spain; I did an internship with a study abroad company in Milan, Italy.

I earned a master's degree in Spanish Applied Linguistics and studied Second Language Acquisition.

It wasn't enough. I was hungry for more travel, more discovery of other cultures.

Finally, I got the chance to move to Barcelona to work. I moved over here in 2002 and planned to stay for two years. I told my family, friends, and girlfriend (at the time) that I would be here for two years and then move back. That was twenty years ago, and ... ummm ... sorry friends.

Since arriving in Barcelona, I have worked directly with American students abroad—teaching culture courses, helping students integrate, guiding students through their internship experience, and creating reentry workshops to discover how to use their experience to get them a job.

I also work as an Intercultural Consultant to executives, from Multinational companies, going through the same challenges I went through.

Now, after working with almost 10,000 students and dozens of executives and enjoying the challenges and extreme fun of a multicultural family, I'm excited to help you.

WHO THIS BOOK IS FOR

This book is for the student looking to get the most out of their study abroad experience, the student who is up for the challenge of learning what is culturally appropriate, and the student who is willing and ready to step out of their comfort zone—again and again.

This book is for students ready to make mistakes, look foolish, and laugh and learn. This is for the student willing to take a chance and participate in the activities I suggest, from start to finish, because THAT student will come out of the experience having gained all of the attributes I mentioned above and more. That student will transform, in incredible ways, and have the time of their life.

I've seen too many students who just go abroad to drink and party. Don't get me wrong; drinking and nightlife can play a role in learning about the culture and yourself. You can bond with the locals while experiencing the nightlife as they do. I did it when I went abroad, and still have great memories of those times.

But, if you want to just hang out with American friends and go to bars with the Americans on the program, let me save you a lot of money and time and suggest that you just stay home.

Bottom line: you could have an incredible experience, personally, professionally, culturally, and academically, or you could not. You could go abroad, and it would be fine, but I want to help you make it unforgettable. I'm assuming you want that, too, which is why I'm so passionate about the tools in this book to help you do that. Keep reading, and you'll see.

MY EXAMPLES IN THIS BOOK

Quick note: the majority of my time abroad has been in Spain, and so most of my examples come from there, but **the tips and strategies I provide in the book are purposefully general enough to apply to any study abroad location**—whether you are in Madrid or Mongolia.

TAKE A CLOSER LOOK

Some of the examples in this book may make you feel uncomfortable in that we are going to hold up a giant mirror to look at ourselves and our own culture in ways you probably have never done before. It's like looking at one of those makeup mirrors that magnifies your pores—it's not always pretty, but in the end, you get a much clearer picture of what you're trying to see.

That giant mirror you will be peering into will make you deeply analyze what you think is right or wrong, cool or uncool, normal or strange, and even ethical or unethical. It will test your deepest assumptions in ways they have never been tested before. This can be difficult and jarring but also necessary as part of the growth process. At times I'll ask you to suspend judgment, even when it's hard and you feel you know you are right. That's ok. Suspending judgment doesn't mean NOT making a judgment; it just means learning to analyze the why behind actions and behaviors first.

This book is about seeing the world from different perspectives and accepting the uncomfortable reality that the way we've seen the world our whole lives might not be the "right" way or, at least, not the only way.

Without question, there are certain universal rights and wrongs—especially when it comes to the treatment of certain people or marginalized identities. Sometimes, when we are in other cultures with a different set of values, our very identities can put us at risk; what has been deemed safe, in our cultural waters, could be dangerous in others. However, the majority of cultural differences students will encounter are not like that, so I will be focusing on what you are most likely to experience while you are abroad. This book will give you new tools to analyze those likely situations—ones in which you may not have found yourself before.

There is another disclaimer that I'd like to state right away, because I can already hear readers saying, "But I don't fit that cultural trait, or I know someone who isn't like that." Of course! When we talk about cultural tendencies, it will never describe every person in that culture. There are regional differences and individual differences, but certainly there are cultural tendencies that belong to groups in general, if not to each and every member. I'm saying that here so I don't have to repeat it throughout the book.

STUDY ABROAD IS A HIGH-IMPACT PRACTICE

What's more high impact than study abroad? It expands our horizons, increases our adaptability, allows us to see the world from different perspectives, makes us more confident and willing to take risks, improves our problem-solving skills, deepens our powers of empathy, and helps us connect with people from around the world who look and sound different than we do.

Study abroad does all this and more for you, if done properly.

Are you ready to take the plunge into new cultural waters?

Chapter 1

WHAT TO KNOW BEFORE YOU GO

SO, YOU'VE DECIDED TO STUDY ABROAD, AND YOU'RE WONDERING WHAT TO EXPECT

Warning!

DON'T EXPECT YOUR EXPERIENCE TO ONLY BE LIKE THE SOCIAL-MEDIA POSTS OF YOUR FRIENDS WHO HAVE BEEN ABROAD! Social media amplifies the best aspects of someone's life and hides the difficult parts.

Take this example: one of my friends posted photos of her and her boyfriend having a picture-perfect candle-lit dinner out at a fancy restaurant, toasting to the camera with their wine glasses and ear-to-ear smiles. Of course, my reaction was, *damn, why are my wife and I just here at home, with our leftovers, watching Netflix once again like every other evening. What's wrong with my relationship?*

But when I talked to that friend the next day, and I mentioned how nice the meal looked, she said, "No, it was terrible. Right after we posted that photo, we got into a huge fight and barely spoke for the rest of the meal and the rest of the night."

It's the same with the posts, photos, videos, and stories that you hear from other students abroad. They only show off the best parts of their experience and hide the difficult and challenging parts.

However, I'll let you in on a secret—**those difficult and challenging experiences turn into the best parts**. They are what help you grow and give you better stories, more than the picture-perfect moments do. It might not feel like it at the time, but believe me; they are.

The confidence you gain when you get through those tough parts—and you will get through them—makes you stronger, more self-assured, more resilient, and more willing to take risks. And you would not gain that strength if everything was easy.

Those transformations you've seen in other students didn't just happen through osmosis; those students worked for them, and they followed tips and strategies that I'll lay out for you in this book.

THIS IS A HUGE INVESTMENT

Study abroad is a big investment:

- **In time.** It takes you away from your school activities, friends, family, and pets.

- **In money.** Study abroad requires cash, not just for the program itself, which may be significant, but also for your flights, travel, day-to-day life, and entertainment. Something important to keep in mind: study abroad does NOT have to be prohibitively expensive. You should speak to your study abroad office about the lower-cost programs out there. There are also scholarships, grants, and several ways to save money and spend wisely. Go to FishinWaterBook.com for more resources.

- **In energy.** As you saw in the introduction, living abroad takes a lot of emotional energy. I like to say that (compared to your everyday life), when you are abroad, the lows are lower, and the highs are higher. One minute you can't manage to use the Italian that you have been studying since high school, to order a simple cappuccino and croissant, and the next minute you meet a local and can miraculously explain, in almost perfect Italian, what you are doing in Rome this semester, and that makes you feel on top of the world!

...BUT THE BENEFITS ARE IMMENSE

The **benefits** that you will reap, both professionally and personally, can pay off in more ways than you ever imagined—if you do it properly. Take it from the millions of study abroad students who came before you.

FIRST THINGS, FIRST

This chapter will outline the steps to take—even before leaving your home country—to help prepare you. So buy yourself a nice journal and grab your favorite pen, or start a new Google Doc, because this is about to get fun. If you're already in-country, don't worry, it's not too late! You can still start now.

YOUR PURPOSE AND GOALS

Before starting with your specific goals, it's time to get a little more philosophical and think about your purpose. Have you ever thought about your purpose in life—where you are headed and what you want to do? Not just *I want to be a psychologist or an entrepreneur*, but *I want to help others get over their trauma*, or *I want to help others achieve their dreams*. Grounding your goals in an overall purpose gives you a better chance to succeed.

→ ACT: Your Purpose

Jot down some ideas of what you feel your purpose or mission in life is. I recognize that this idea feels "heavy," and maybe too "touchy-feely," or just something you've never really thought of before. If so, don't worry; you can skip this for now and go straight to the goals. One great thing about study abroad is that we have more time to be philosophical about these things, and we experience so many challenges that force us to have these deeper thoughts. So, if you are not in the mood to do it right now, don't worry; it will probably happen, without you even realizing, while you're abroad.

→ ACT: Your Goals DRAFT

Take ten minutes to write down all of the goals for your time abroad, and don't read ahead yet! This will be your first draft.

Now that you have written them, how do they look to you? Are you inspired? If not, that's okay; we will work on them together now.

YOUR HOBBIES FROM BACK HOME

Did you include in your goals carrying on with hobbies that you do back home? What are your favorite hobbies—the ones you'd be upset not to continue during your time abroad? Is it yoga, going to movies, baking, playing soccer, jogging, playing guitar, or singing in a band?

Finding a way to continue those hobbies in your new host country is going to be one of the best ways to combat culture shock, meet loads of new people, find out how the locals do what you do, etc.

When I wanted to give up and quit my new job and my commitment, one of the few things that helped turn my mood around was taking salsa classes. It turned into THE MAIN THING I looked forward to every week. I became friends with the other people. I ended up meeting them out for drinks or meals, outside of class, and dancing together on the weekends.

It gave me some of the essential tricks and a roadmap to keep me going and growing:

- Meet new people
- Get exercise
- Push me out of my comfort zone
- Give me some challenges to overcome

That's a very good, quick, and easy roadmap for you. But there is much more to come…

WHAT IS SOMETHING NEW YOU WANT TO LEARN ABOUT?

Going abroad gives you a fresh start and a chance to learn something new! This could be academic or not. Some examples could be learning about entrepreneurship in London, winemaking in Tuscany, didgeridoo in Australia, how to make Pilsner beer in Prague, or Muay Thai martial-arts classes in Thailand.

Think of it this way: what's more exciting as a souvenir and memory of your time abroad, buying a trinket that sits on your shelf or taking home a new skill that you'll have for the rest of your life?

WHAT ARE SMART GOALS?

You may have heard the idea of SMART goals before. If not, this is as good a time as any to learn about them, because you will hear all about them, in the professional world, soon enough. SMART goals are widely used in the business world, or for personal growth, and come from George Doran, Arthur Miller, and James Cunningham in their 1981 article "There's a S.M.A.R.T. Way to Write Management Goals and Objectives."[1]

SMART is an acronym that stands for:

- **S**pecific
- **M**eaningful
- **A**chievable
- **R**ealistic or **R**each
- **T**ime bound

Let's break them down, and you can compare the goals that you've written, to see if they fit:

Specific—Instead of saying, "I want to get to know the locals," a more specific goal would be, "I want to meet at least two locals who I can call, at any time, to meet up, and who I keep in touch with once I leave." The idea is that you can easily say whether you achieved it or not.

---

1   George T. Doran, "There's a S.M.A.R.T. Way to Write Management's Goals and Objectives," *Management Review*. 1981, 70 (11): 35–36, https://doi.org/info:doi/.

Meaningful—It's no use making a goal if it's not going to be meaningful to you. Making a goal that is really for others or because you think you are supposed to do it will be harder to achieve. So what is something you can do, while abroad, that will have meaning to you now or in the future?

Achievable—I've had this exchange with so many students who are on a semester program (or even a month-long program):

Student: I want to become fluent in Spanish this term.

Me: What level are you at right now?

Student: I just finished lower-intermediate level.

Me: It's not going to happen.

You CAN improve your language abilities tremendously while abroad (see activities about tips and tricks to improve your language, in Chapter 8), but expecting to become fluent in a short time is not typically achievable.

Realistic or **R**each—Since **R**ealistic is very similar to achievable, I suggest making one of your goals a **R**each goal. In other words, what is one thing that, if you did it, would stretch you as a person beyond anything you thought you could do? Maybe it's to travel by yourself for a weekend, play on a local sports team, or go on one date a month with a local. It's okay not to get to 100 percent of your Reach goal, because many times, even getting to 60 percent, 70 percent, or 80 percent still feels like a huge win.

Timebound—The very fact that your study abroad experience has a clear start and end date makes it time-bound, which is perfect. I got to know all the cities I studied or interned in intimately, because I knew the clock was ticking. I was only in St. Petersburg, Russia, for eight weeks, but I knew the city better than I knew Chicago—the city I grew up just outside of. Make every moment count, while you are abroad, because the time will fly by. Almost every student I've worked with—whether they are abroad for two weeks or four months—remarks on how the time passes much more quickly than they ever imagined.

➔» FAST TRACK ACT: WRITE AND SHARE YOUR UPDATED SMART GOALS

Step 1: Write down your new list of SMART Goals. Remember to think about hobbies from back home and new things you want to learn, and if you can connect them to your purpose, that's a big bonus.

Step 2: Share your ideas with friends. Research tells us that it's easier to commit to something when you've written it down *and* told others about it.

Step 3: Once you have your list, start researching how to do these things in your new city, or ask your program if they can help you do them.

There is a great website and app called Meetup (Meetup.com) where people can form groups and find like-minded people to do activities together. With just a quick search now, I found running clubs in Berlin, sunrise yoga in Buenos Aires, and Bachata in Barcelona.

→ ACT: Set Up a Vivid Action Plan

Now that you have written your SMART goals, it's time to put together a vivid plan of action. I throw in the word "vivid" so you think specifically when and where you will do the *what* of your goals and *who* will help you as a resource.

For example, suppose you said that you want to go to a gym twice a week, as one of your goals; your vivid action plan could state:

One month before the program starts, I will ask my program advisor if they recommend any specific gyms in the city; then I will see if they have any student discounts. My goal is to get to the gym at least once during the first week, then twice a week after that. I'll go between my Art History and my Language and Culture classes on Tuesdays and Thursdays.

QUICK CULTURAL NOTE ABOUT GYMS

Gyms are a fantastic source of cultural information and avenue for cultural immersion. You can meet people, observe how people interact, see the differences in how people work out, and use that as a great excuse to start talking to someone new.

→ ACT: Write "The Future Me Letter"

Remember that letter I wrote to mom that saved me from giving up? It's your turn to write it. I'm not saying that you will feel like giving up and going home before the time is over (although in my experience, about 3 percent of semester-long students do that, and in some cases for very good reasons), but it's helpful to write the letter anyway, and you'll see why.

Write to your parents, best friend, significant other, or your dog. It doesn't matter who you are writing it to; just get pen on paper (or letters on screen), and get ready to pour a little of your heart out. Here's the framework I would suggest, but feel free to change it up to fit your situation.

Dear X,

I'm doing it! I'm going to [city, country] for [duration of the program]. I'm so excited that I made this decision. Did you know that only about 8 percent of students study abroad? That puts me up there with a select group, and I want to make sure I make the most of it.

I will do my best to follow the steps in the book Like a Fish in Water: How to Grow Abroad When You Go Abroad and actively participate, to make this the most rewarding experience possible.

I know that overall it's going to be an incredible time in my life, but I also know there will be tough moments. Please be ready for me to call, write, or message you at some of the low points—the hard times. I know that going through the challenges will be GOOD FOR ME. Most of the time, I will just want you to listen. Don't try to solve things for me. Part of this process is me figuring out things for myself. It's going to be hard, but I can do it.

While I'm away, I hope to continue to [write down your hobbies and interests here].

There are some other things I want to do, like [write down your other goals here.]

I expect the hardest part will be [fill in the blank].

I am most looking forward to [fill in the blank].

I think the thing I'll miss most from home is [fill in the blank].

However, one thing I WON'T miss from home is [fill in the blank, but note: this is not a good time to finish this sentence with "YOU!" and insult the person you are writing to. See the next point].

P.S. Please put more money in my bank account, so I can have some great cultural experiences. ☺ Remember, it's the best investment in my future!

DECISION TIME: CHOOSE YOUR HOUSING

Now that you have thought about your purpose, determined your goals, and started to get into the proper mindset, it's time to think about your housing abroad. Why? The choice of your housing will directly affect the experience you have.

Most programs will give you three or four main options, with some offering more. Let's look at all the pros and cons and how the decision will affect your experience.

→ The Homestay

A homestay usually means living with a local "family," where family could be a husband, wife, and two kids with a dog; a single woman; or any combination of those.

My recommendation to almost all students is to choose a homestay. I did it during my semester in Madrid, for a few weeks in Russia, for a week in Mexico, several weeks in the Philippines, and for a couple days in Morocco.

I gained language skills, learned how to cook local food, got help on my homework, and asked all of my cultural and logistical questions, and—let's not forget—they did my laundry and cooked for me. They also cared for me if I wasn't feeling well, so it was like having a family away from home.

Some students are worried that they won't have the same freedom in a homestay, but most of the ones I know about give you the keys the first day and say come and go as you please (with respect, of course).

One challenge presented by this option could include exhaustion, at times, from having to speak a foreign language and navigate cultural differences 24/7. Speaking a foreign language is like working out—you need to push yourself, but then you need to give your muscles a break before going back to it.

For me, and 90 percent of the students I've worked with who lived in a homestay, this is the best option for those who want to improve their language, learn more about the culture, and feel a bit spoiled.

There are other good options as well:

→ Living in an Apartment with Local Students or Young Professionals

The benefits are similar to a homestay but probably without the laundry and meals included.

I did this during my internship in Milan, and it was a fantastic experience. It was me and three guys about my age. I learned how to make a perfect pasta sauce from them and what they do for fun, got to meet all of their friends, and practiced my Italian nonstop.

This is a great choice if you want the benefits of language and cultural immersion and want to spend time with people closer to you in age.

These could become your new best friends, or there is a chance that you may not get along with them, whereas, in a family (in my experience), that is rarely an issue.

→ Living in an Apartment with Other Students on the Program

The greatest drawback to this option is that there is no cultural or language immersion inherent in the housing itself. However, studies have shown that students in apartments with other students on the program can still get a lot out of the experience when they use their roommates as sounding boards to reflect on what they are experiencing.

For example, if everyone you live with is reading this book, and you talk about the challenges and activities that I suggest, there is a huge benefit to that shared reflection.

Another issue with this option is the same as the last one: your roommates could become your best friends, or there is a chance that you won't get along with them, and you might have someone who breaks the rules, gets you in trouble, or just annoys the hell out of you.

As you'll see later in this book, even that problem could be seen as a positive, in that you will have to learn conflict resolution, a very handy life skill.

→ Living in a Residence Hall

The terms residence hall or dorm can mean many different things around the world, so it's hard to generalize here, but if you can find an option to live in a residence hall, with other local or international students, with ample opportunity to mix with them, this could be a top option as well. Depending on what type it is, you may get the language practice and the chance to get tips on the local city and culture, and if you are with other international students, the opportunity to learn about other countries and cultures is a huge bonus.

Ok, now that you've done some pre-departure prep, it's time to start going deeper. In the next chapter, I'll tell you about Cultural Autopilot and why it's so important for you to learn how to adjust it.

DIVE DEEPER INTO...

→ Preparation prior to departure:

Steven T. Duke, *Preparing to Study Abroad: Learning to Cross Cultures* (Sterling: Stylus Publishing, LLC, 2014).

→ The ills and dangers of social media:

Jeff Orlowski, dir. *The Social Dilemma*. Exposure Labs/Netflix, 2020, https://www.netflix.com/search?q=the%20social&jbv=81254224.

→ Research into student learning abroad:

Michael Vande Berg, Jeffrey Connor-Linton, and R. Michael Paige. 2009 "The Georgetown Consortium Project: Interventions for Student Learning Abroad." *Frontiers: The Interdisciplinary Journal of Study Abroad* 18 (1): 1-75. https://doi.org/10.36366/frontiers.v18i1.251.

Chapter 2

LIVING ON
CULTURAL AUTOPILOT

WHAT THE HELL IS WATER?

What does this comic strip have to do with culture? Why does one fish have to ask what water is even though they are swimming around in it their whole lives?

We are just like that fish in the water—swimming around in our own culture without even realizing that we are in it. What happens when you pluck a fish out of water? It starts flopping around wildly, realizing that something is very wrong, and questioning what the hell is going on here. They know—they *feel*—that something's not right.

The reason it can be so jarring is that, when we are in our own culture and haven't yet experienced anything too different, we are living in what I like to call **Cultural Autopilot**. How people will react to our behavior isn't something that requires a lot of thought or effort on our part. We know how to communicate, how to fit in, and what will make us stick out; we do what we grew up knowing to be "true" and "right" and "polite."

THE PROTAGONIST OF THIS BOOK—CULTURE

We've been talking so much about this word, culture, but we haven't even defined it yet. What is culture, and why is it such a fascinating thing to study? Let's start with some definitions. There are loads of different definitions out there, and many of them are more academic than the ones I like to use. Let's look at my favorite two.

"Culture is what is expected, reinforced, and rewarded within a particular social group."
　　　　—Jörg Schmitz, Business Anthropologist

When we are in our own cultural waters, we are on Cultural Autopilot in our everyday lives: moving, doing, acting, and speaking in ways that we rarely have to intentionally think about. When you need to buy a single bottle of water, you know you can jump in your car or walk to the nearest shop, find the bottle of water that you need, grab it off the shelf, and take it to the register; you know how to wait in line, how to pay for it, whether to say thank you or not, and what to do if anything goes wrong.

Seems simple enough, right?

Take this true story of one of my friends from Barcelona, who was traveling in the US. She went into a big grocery store and wanted a bottle of water, but only one. The only bottles of water she found were in plastic-wrapped packs of six units. So she did what she does back home; she ripped open the pack and took a bottle of water. When she got to the register to pay, the clerk was outraged and yelled at her.

When she defended herself, saying that this is what they do where she shops (back in Barcelona), she was not forgiven; she had to buy the whole, now broken, six-pack.

The clerk's response was not what she **expected**, and her behavior was certainly not **reinforced** or **rewarded**. In fact, it was punished. And when we go to live in other cultures, these "cultural incidents" happen to us, all the time, until we learn what the "right way" to act is.

Culture is: what we do around here, now. This definition is vague, but I love it, and it comes in handy very often when a student encounters one of these cultural incidents that makes them stop in their tracks and think: what is going on? We ask ourselves that because cultural rules are often unwritten. But we just know—we *feel*—that something is right or wrong. We either feel like we fit in or stick out.

These cultural incidents don't have to be borderline shoplifting like the example above. When studying in Madrid, I went to a café with my host mother for breakfast one morning. She let me order first, so I said, in the best Spanish I had learned in school and was proud to show off: *"Yo quisiera un café con leche por favor."* ("I would like a coffee with milk, please.") The waiter looked at me sideways and laughed but took my order. Then he turned to my host mom, and she said, *"Ponme un café con leche y un croissant."* ("Give me a coffee with milk and a croissant.")

I felt comfortable enough with her to say, "Isn't it sort of rude to just bark orders at the waiter, speak so directly, and not even say please?!" She said, "This is just the way we order around here. You don't say 'I would like' or even 'please.' It's not what we do."

I felt like a fish out of water. What I thought was right was instantaneously rejected and replaced with something that I deeply felt was wrong.

Traveling to other cultures strongly highlights **when** we stick out and don't fit in—but it's the **why** we stick out and don't fit in that fascinates me. Let me introduce you to the simple and brilliant tool that helps us do that.

MEET THE CULTURAL ICEBERG

I know the metaphor of the iceberg is probably overused. However, it's the perfect, simple, yet highly effective metaphor that we can utilize to help you see your world from a different perspective and adapt to your new surroundings.

If you are already abroad, you have undoubtedly noticed things that are different to you, things that make you stop and think: *that's interesting,* or *you'd never see that where I come from.* Those observations are gold! **They are the explicit, visible aspects of culture above the water.**

Below the water's surface lies so much more—the why behind what we do, what is implicit and often invisible that drives our behaviors.

→ "Let's Iceberg That"

We will now take this metaphor to a new level—we will turn iceberg into a verb.

This **new verb:** "To iceberg" is a term I invented to mean:
to first observe a cultural behavior, or some aspect of a culture,
then dive deeper and find out what the values and beliefs are that
make people act that way.

Or simply:

to find out why people do the things they do and act the way they act.

We will be doing a lot of iceberging in this book, so be prepared.

Note: An iceberg sometimes conjures up an image of danger and destruction, but that's not what we are going for here. Instead, think majestic beauty and the great unknown below the water, waiting to be discovered.

I like iceberg as a verb, because it shows us that it is an action that takes work and energy. It's not a static noun that we just look at passively. To run with that, getting the most out of this experience will not just happen to you passively; it will take effort.

→ So How Do You Iceberg?

The idea is simple, but it's not always easy.

The first step is to observe some aspect of the culture. What is something that's visible, explicit? Basically, it's something that you observe and describe without ascribing an interpretation or analysis of any kind.

Let's look at some examples from my own travels:

- In Spain, most stores close on Sundays.

- When I traveled to Copenhagen, an American friend of mine pointed out how many parents often leave their babies in strollers, outside of restaurants in the cold, while they eat inside.

- In Russia, people on the street generally don't smile at strangers.

- In Italy, many people tend to gesticulate with their hands when speaking.

- In the US, people generally arrive before the scheduled times for meetings.

Notice that I am qualifying these sentences with "many," "most," or "generally." That's because there will always be exceptions to cultural tendencies, and at this stage, you are just observing, so it's especially dangerous to say "all people" or "they always."

Also, none of those sentences are followed by: "…because they think that" or "…and that's so strange or wrong." That's because we are not interpreting or evaluating yet. If you catch yourself making judgments, that's okay right now—it is very difficult to simply observe and describe without judging! Just take note of it and try to correct yourself.

Here's a real example of me breaking this rule when I studied in Madrid. Can you spot where I went beyond observation and started judging? Here is how it went down:

Me (to a Spanish friend I met in one of my classes): I've noticed that there is a lot of PDA here in Madrid.

Her: What is PDA?

Me: Public displays of affection.

Her: What does that mean?

Me: You know, when two people are doing things in public that really should be done in private and you want to yell, "Get a room!"

Her: Like what?

Me: Like kissing, hugging a little too close, groping, straddling each other...

Her: What's wrong with doing that in public?

Me: [Wow, mind blown.]

Can you spot the observations versus the judgment?

Here, my only true observations were that I saw people kissing. Everything else had judgment seeped into it.

"Hugging a little too close ..." A little too close is from my cultural perspective. Someone else would not necessarily see it as "too close."

"Groping" implies a negative connotation.

Even the word "straddling" is laced with judgment as opposed to saying, "sitting on top of each other."

As I said, it's really hard to separate the judgment from the observation.

WHAT'S NEW TO YOU?

It's your turn to practice the first step of iceberging.

Within twenty-four hours of arriving in the new country, and pretty much every time I see them after that, I like to ask students, "What's new to you?" "What sticks out as strange or different or something that makes you stop and say, 'Wow, you wouldn't see that where I come from'?" These questions pull you out of Cultural Autopilot and make you take notice and gather the cultural material above the water.

➔» FAST TRACK ACT: WHAT'S NEW TO YOU?

Step 1: If you are abroad already, take a few minutes now to write down everything that has stuck out to you as new or different.

Were you able to come up with many? I guarantee that the longer you are abroad and the more you sharpen your observation skills, the longer your list will be.

Were you able to do it without making a judgment? Remember that observations are just statements or descriptions devoid of any interpretation or evaluation. If you found yourself making a judgment, don't worry; for now, just note it down. You'll be able to compare these early observations to ones you make later when you are more practiced.

Step 2: Talk to other non-locals, share your ideas with them, and see if they noticed these differences too.

Step 3: Run your ideas past someone from the host culture, and see how they react to your observations. Be especially careful not to make JUDGMENTS here, just observations.

→ The Next Step: Diving below the Water

As we saw in one of the definitions above, culture is what we do around here, now. However, we can't just stop there and say, *this is what we do*. We can go deeper, and that's where the iceberg comes in—to think about *why we do what we do around here, now*.

The next step is to determine the values and beliefs that drive that behavior.

→ How Do We Discover What's under the Water?

Let's begin with this example: why are stores closed on Sundays in Spain? What values and beliefs do they hold that lead to that behavior? We have to dive deeper to find this out. Where Step 1 is explicit and visible, Step 2 is implicit and often invisible or unwritten and, therefore, takes more time and work to discover—but that's the fun part.

My experience and research have shown me which Spanish values and beliefs lead many stores to be closed on Sundays. Spanish values include enjoying free time with family and friends, practicing some hobby, traveling, having a long lunch, and just not working all the time. The value of that extra money they could make on Sunday isn't worth giving up these other values. Plus, to keep shops open, you should have shoppers, right? If Spaniards don't tend to want to shop on a Sunday, in order to take advantage of their free time, then those shops would be empty.

I've learned this through talking to many locals, asking the right questions, and studying Spain's history, through books, films, guided tours, etc. These are some of the basics to help you learn what is below the water's surface, wherever you are studying. The other chapters and activities in this book will also provide more guidance.

The other beauty of iceberging is that it allows us to learn more about ourselves. Why did it shock me that stores were closed on Sundays? In the US, stores are not only open on Sundays, but they often have expanded hours, sometimes 24/7. Sundays are a day to get shopping done, because we work the other days, and our work is immensely important.

Values in the US include being productive (we like to get things done—which could even include shopping and checking those things off our to-do list), and we value having stuff—new house, car, etc.—because it helps to show status. We value hard work, which leads to money, which allows us to buy that stuff. Shopping is a pastime; going to the malls on the weekend is something to do. And finally, we love convenience and the ability to get what we want, when we want it, which is the opposite of wanting to buy something on a Sunday and seeing "closed" signs on all of the stores.

→ Suspend Judgment—Change Your Perspective

I want to drive home this idea that we shouldn't be interpreting, evaluating, or judging these cultural behaviors that stick out to us until we fully understand the *why* behind them.

When I first came to live in Spain and, wanting to get my shopping done on Sundays, encountered all the stores closed, my reaction was absolutely: *this is so stupid. Why wouldn't stores be open today?! I want to spend my money, and they don't want to take it. If they just worked a little more, they could make more money.* I don't think I used (or at least I hope I didn't) the "lazy" word in my judgment, but I probably wasn't far off.

Now I've changed, and I look forward to a Sunday where I CAN'T shop and, instead, spend my time with family or do leisure activities.

When we iceberg (and generally when we cross cultures) it's incredibly important to just observe, first, with no judgment, but it took me a while to learn that.

OUR WORDS MATTER

As you can see in the earlier examples, our words matter tremendously. If we don't want to offend other cultures, we must choose our words carefully. There are a handful of words to especially watch out for:

→ 1. Normal

A DANGEROUS WORD IN CULTURAL STUDIES

I often have students ask me: "Where can I get a normal cup of coffee?" or "Where can I buy a normal notebook?" These are great questions that make me laugh, when I hear them, because they are indicative of our cultural lenses. Of course, what is normal to us is not always normal to someone else.

A "normal" cup of coffee, a "normal" distance to stand apart when talking to someone, and a "normal" time to eat dinner all mean something very different to different cultures.

→ 2. Polite and Rude

My own example of ordering coffee with, "I would like a coffee with milk please," and finding it "rude" when my host mom ordered hers in a way that was "impolite" to me shows my cultural blunder. Or if I considered it polite to smile at strangers and, therefore, found Russians rude for not smiling, I was ascribing a judgment to something I didn't fully understand at the time.

→ 3. Right and Wrong

Many parents (and even non-parents!) might think it's wrong to leave your baby napping in the stroller, outside a restaurant, in freezing temperatures, while you eat inside, but that's what many parents in Denmark and Norway do. Not just that, but Norwegians contend it has health benefits and, therefore, actually believe it's a good thing to do.

We will continue this thread of interpreting normal, polite, rude, right, and wrong throughout the rest of this book. In the meantime, in your day-to-day life, I suggest you keep a record—written is best, but at least a mental note—of what sticks out to you as abnormal, rude, or wrong in your new culture abroad. I also recommend keeping note of the behaviors that seem similar to you, which you would have anticipated to be different.

I suggest a written record so you'll have something concrete to look back at later, when you reflect on what you've learned; and it will come in handy when we talk about how to use this experience to make you more employable. The more specific anecdotes you have, the better, and I guarantee you will be happy that you wrote them down!

INTERCULTURAL COMPETENCE (ICC) PART I

Adaptability helps people gain what the cultural gurus claim is one of the most important skills of a global leader: Intercultural Competence (also known as ICC). One of the many definitions of ICC is *the ability to understand the values and beliefs behind behavior and reconcile them with your own.*

Let's break that down:

→ 1. The Ability to Understand the Values and Beliefs behind Behavior

If only we had a tool to do that. Oh, yes, iceberging. When we iceberg a behavior, we dive deep to understand the values and beliefs that drive that behavior. Learning to iceberg is like working out; you need to practice to get better and better. So, let's work those muscles and set you on a path to become an expert iceberger.

→ 2. ...and Reconcile Them with Your Own (Values and Beliefs)

We've only just started talking about this idea of understanding yourself and your own culture, but we will go much deeper into it in Chapter 3.

We can't wrap up this chapter about our Cultural Autopilot without mentioning the dreaded: CULTURE SHOCK.

CULTURE SHOCK

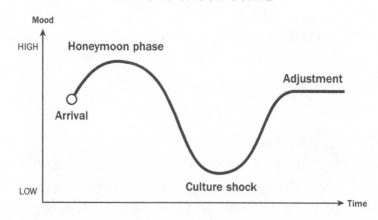

Based on Oberg (1960) and Gallhorn & Gallhorn (1963)

Bum, buumm, buuuuum. The dreaded culture shock! Culture shock could be defined as a feeling of disorientation and an overwhelming mix of negative emotions when your expectations of life vary greatly from reality. Maybe you've even seen the typical Culture Shock W or U Curve. It looks like a fun roller coaster until you look more closely and see that you will reach the depths of despair, and be forced to confront deeper issues because of the mismatch of your expectations compared to what life is really like.

This graph is not used much anymore because it seems too prescriptive. That is, not every person who goes abroad will hit these major highs and major lows, or they might, but not in this order.

So let's scrap that roller coaster in favor of another graph I like better—the Cultural Coil—which demonstrates ups and downs, without a timeline, and a repetitive cycle that eventually ends up higher than where it started.

CULTURE SHOCK COIL

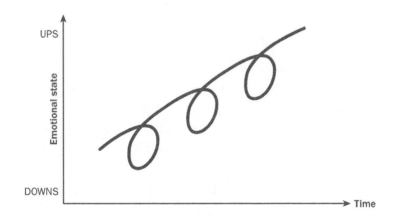

Let's take this real-life example:

Sofia is a student who studied French for six years, got straight As throughout college so far, then, in her first week in Paris, realizes that she can't understand anyone—not even her homestay mom—because they speak a lot faster than her teacher back home. She gets massively lost because she takes the wrong bus and arrives an hour late to orientation. At lunch, she orders what she thinks is a vegetarian dish, but it has meat, so she doesn't eat it, and the server is very "rude to her" because she didn't eat it and can't explain herself. In reality, the server is asking why she didn't like it and if she would like something else, but she doesn't understand and is so frustrated, at that point, she just wants to give up.

One of my students summed it up like this: "I know I'm smart, but I felt like an idiot at times."

But let's refer back to that coil and see how things can look up. The next day Sofia gets to class on time with a flawless execution of public transport; she gets a little lost but asks for, and receives, directions in French and understands them perfectly; she orders the most delicious vegetarian dish she's ever tasted and even gets a smile from the server. Best day ever! Accomplishing all of that back home would be an average day, nothing special, but doing it all in another culture and country is a herculean feat to be proud of.

I always say that, when we are abroad, the highs are higher, and the lows are lower—sometimes all in one day.

One of the best ways to stave off those lows is to prepare yourself for them. Another way is to enjoy them and learn from them; look forward to the shock!

The next chapter will tell us if you are ready for the challenge.

DIVE DEEPER INTO...

→ Culture shock:

Dianne Hofner Saphiere, "The Nasty (and Noble) Truth About Culture Shock," *Cultural Detective Blog*, August 12, 2014, https://blog.culturaldetective.com/2014/08/12/the-nasty-and-noble-truth-about-culture-shock/.

"Cultural Adaptation Culture Shock," NAFSA, May 14, 2010, https://www.nafsa.org/professional-resources/browse-by-interest/cultural-adaptation-culture-shock.

Chapter 3

YOU HAVE TO ADAPT TO THE CULTURE BECAUSE IT WON'T ADAPT TO YOU

When I first moved to Barcelona to work, I thought I had it all under control; I was ready for anything! And why wouldn't I be? By that point, I had studied abroad in Russia (Russia!) and spent a semester in Madrid, where I took all classes in Spanish (plus a Russian class at a Spanish university). I had lived and worked in Milan, for a summer, and I had led two groups of high-school students separately throughout Spain.

I WAS READY FOR ANYTHING, I THOUGHT

Yet time after time, little cultural differences started to slowly get to me, and big things got to me quickly. I was annoyed and confounded that:

- They walked so slowly. *Didn't they have places to go, things to do, and people to see?!*

- I'd go into a restaurant with six friends at 7:00 p.m., ready to sit down for a nice, long dinner, and the staff would shoo us away and say, "Sorry, we don't open until 8:30 p.m." *What?! Fine, I'll take my money somewhere else, and that will show them.*

- People were so **rude**. When I spoke, they would constantly talk over me and not even let me finish my sentence before they butted in. *Don't they know what polite conversation is?*

- I would plan to meet someone—whether at work or casually—and they would always be late. Then, when they finally arrived, there were no apologies. They had wasted my time and didn't have the decency to even acknowledge it. *How rude!*

These seemingly small frustrations made me quietly withdraw, at times, and blow up in anger at other times, neither of which has ever been a part of my character. Sometimes I didn't recognize myself.

Until one day, when I complained about these cultural differences to my boss from Barcelona and he said something that pissed me off but was the best advice he could have given me. Some cold, hard love. He said, "Rich, you have to adapt to the culture; the culture is not going to adapt to you."

My first response was to think: *your culture sucks, and it should be more like mine. My culture knows how to do business, doesn't rudely interrupt people, doesn't waste other people's time, and provides conveniences. And who doesn't like—no—who doesn't NEED convenience?!*

But looking back on it now, my boss was right, and my attitude was wrong. Culture is so ingrained in people that I'm not going to change their culture. What was I thinking?

I know what I was thinking; I was cocky and arrogant because, after my experiences, I thought I knew it all. And coming from the United States of America, I've had it drilled into me that we are the best country in the world. Just listen to almost any US politician speak, and you'll see what I mean.

Mostly, I was suffering from culture shock, and when you are in the downward spiral of the dreaded culture-shock coil, it's hard to see clearly, which means it's easy to become defensive, combative, withdrawn, and feisty. It was easier, and it felt comforting to only see things from my point of view.

I needed help to see things from the other perspective, a skill I later gained, which helped me tremendously—not just in adapting abroad but also in work and life in general.

QUIZ: DO YOU HAVE WHAT IT TAKES?

Before we go any further, we will find out if you have what it takes to succeed abroad, with a simple quiz! That's right; this ninety-second quiz will let you know whether you will succeed or fail, terribly, when you embark on your journey. Let's find out, shall we?

Here's how this works:

- Don't turn the page yet!

- Don't start until I tell you to.

- When you start, you will see sixteen math problems to solve as fast as you can.

- Do not use a calculator.

- Set a timer for yourself for ninety seconds. That is all you get.

- When you finish all the problems, or ninety seconds are up, put your pen down and don't go back and change anything.

A couple of last notes: I have done this activity with well over 1,000 students and the record for the fastest time was thirty-three seconds done by an engineering student from the University of Texas at Austin. Can you beat that?

Okay, ready; turn the page and go!

Global Competence: 50 Training Activities for Succeeding in International Business

Working in Unfamiliar Surroundings: Quiz

What follows are some simple arithmetic problems. Therefore, it should be easy for you to get the correct answers. However, you are in a different country and the symbols for multiplication, addition, division, and subtraction follow a different logic. They are as follows:

−	means to multiply
÷	means to add
+	means to divide
X	means to subtract

Instructions

1. *Complete the problems on the right, following the above instructions.*

2. *Do not change the signs on the paper.*

3. *Put the results in the appropriate boxes.*

4. *When finished, hold your hand up for a moment to tell me that you are done.*

5. *Hurry! You will be timed!*

8 − 2 =	☐	9 + 1 =	☐
12 + 4 =	☐	5 − 6 =	☐
4 x 3 =	☐	2 x 1 =	☐
6 ÷ 2 =	☐	10 + 5 =	☐
9 ÷ 3 =	☐	12 − 2 =	☐
7 x 4 =	☐	6 − 6 =	☐
4 − 2 =	☐	8 − 5 =	☐
8 + 4 =	☐	6 ÷ 6 =	☐
12 x 2 =	☐	17 x 2 =	☐
20 + 10 =	☐	14 − 7 =	☐

Done! How did you do? And when I ask, how did you do, I don't actually care about the answers. Well, that's not exactly true; if you answered "6" for the first one, then I do care, because you did it incorrectly, and your answers don't count. It means that you solved the problems with the wrong rules.

There are three questions that I care about:

1. How did you FEEL during this activity? When I ask the students I work with, I inevitably get the answers:

   a. Frustrated

   b. Stressed

   c. Challenged

   d. Happy—enjoyed the challenge

   e. Slow

   f. Foolish (especially the ones who didn't do the new rules and finished the test in twenty seconds, thinking they were awesome)

2. What is the purpose of this test, and what does it have to do with going abroad?

3. What discoveries can it tell you about living in other cultures?

Take a minute to write down your answers.

If you said, "It's to show me that when I go abroad, the rules (the *rules of culture*), are going to be different than what I'm used to. It's sometimes hard to remember what to do; your own ingrained rules slow you down and get in the way, causing mistakes, meaning others may see me as less intelligent or less competent, and all of that will make me feel frustrated, stressed, challenged, slow and foolish, and maybe happy if I like the challenge," then you're exactly right!

Here are some more questions for you about that activity:

- If the rules were your "normal" rules of arithmetic, would you have had the same feelings about it? Probably not.

- Would it have stressed you out and frustrated you? Probably not.

- Would you have finished it a lot faster? Most definitely, yes.

- Would you have learned anything from it? Probably not.

Had that activity been with the rules you are used to, you could have almost done it all without thinking. Taking that test with the normal rules is like living in our own culture, just like that fish swimming in its usual waters on Cultural Autopilot. Once we are out of those waters, what's automatic in our culture would not be automatic in another, and that's when we feel thrown off.

This might be how you are feeling right now. That's ok! Don't try to prevent yourself from feeling frustrated and stressed, because those feelings, and more importantly, the experiences that lead to those feelings, will help you grow and learn.

You should be prepared and eager to feel like a fool and out of your depth sometimes. I know this is easier said than done.

I'm only saying this from a position of authority, now, because I've felt the fool myself hundreds of times. If my past self or some of my past bosses were to learn that I was the one to help you through this, there might be laughter or even incredulity.

Let me explain:

SUKA STORY

Here's the story of one of my (many) major failures while abroad that taught me a great lesson. When I went to study in St. Petersburg, I had only taken four semesters of Russian, so I could speak decently but definitely not at an advanced level. I felt confident and brave, though, and ready for some challenges, so I decided to go to the store, by myself, to buy some orange juice. Big moment, right?

At that time in Russia, I didn't find a grocery store that was similar to the ones I was used to in the US, where you walk down each aisle, calmly grabbing what you want, drop it into your cart, then go to the register to pay with a credit card, barely having to interact with anyone. Oh no, this was a full-on test of my inter-cultural and linguistic ability.

There were workers (a few younger women) behind the store counter with all the products behind them. You walk up to the counter and tell them what you want (not a lick of English was spoken, and there were no products with English writing), they give it to you, then you take it to the cashier to pay.

I walked up to the counter as confidently as possible but, in a small voice, said: *Dobray dien* (good morning), *Xotel bouyoo* (I would like) *suka*. The woman behind the counter was not smiling. Even though I knew this was "normal" in Russia (see Chapter 10), it was still unnerving because not only was she not smiling, she had a very confused look on her face and said *Shtoo?* (What?). So I tried another tactic; forget the pleasantries and go straight to what I was looking for: *suka*. More confusion, and the other women working there stopped and watched the situation unfold. At this point, my blood was rising along with the temperature in the room, my defenses were up, and I thought, I better just point and say the word louder. So I pointed at the juice behind her and almost pleaded *suka*!

This worked. Success! The other woman gingerly grabbed the juice and handed it to me. I walked to the register, took out my rubles, with shaking hands, and headed straight back to ask my director what had happened in this cultural incident.

I explained to him what had occurred. He gave me a knowing look and said, "The word for juice is *sok*, not wha–t you said." I couldn't believe it and replied, "Yeah but *sok—suka*. There is not much difference. And we are in the store, and the juice was right behind her. Couldn't she get it from the context?" (See how I shifted the blame here from me to her? Definitely not a positive trait for successful overseas living.)

The director said, "Yeah, well, *suka* means...slut."

In fact, the dictionary definition is worse: slut, hooker, harlot, prostitute, tart. Nooo!! I was so mortified that I had insulted this woman, even though it was completely unintended.

One thing that I learned about myself, from that incredibly cringe-worthy, embarrassing situation, was that I had a hard time keeping calm and keeping a sense of humor, when I was in a stressful situation, especially if other people were insinuating that I was making a mistake. That critical incident threw me into a fight-or-flight response as a defense mechanism blocking my normal reaction, which would have been to calmly think things through.

Fortunately for me, I have become much better at this after all of my experiences abroad. Fortunately for you, there is no shortage of opportunities to practice this while abroad because, believe me, you will make mistakes, and you will experience failures...hopefully!

REFRAMING FAILURE

As a result of my cultural mishaps and mistakes, I learned to reframe failure into a learning experience. If you search Amazon books right now and type in "failure," there are over 16,000 results; filtering down to just search in self-help books, you still get over 4,000 results. That's because learning to use failure as a way to grow is so important, especially from an American cultural lens.

To turn failures into the learning opportunities we are hoping for, we need to have the proper mindsets. I say "mindsets," plural, because there are several that we need.

→ Mindsets

How do you get through those failures and come out stronger on the other side? Study abroad is like many things in life: **you will get out of it as much as you put into it**. The tricky thing is, getting the most out of it, when you are swimming in other cultures, is not easy.

These next few paragraphs just might change your life. Almost every time I talk to students about growth mindset, someone comes back to me and says it was exactly what they needed to hear. Two weeks after one presentation, a student wrote this to me: "I haven't stopped thinking about what you said about growth mindset and fixed mindset. I stop myself every time I hear the fixed mindset voice in my head, and I try to turn it around. Thank you for introducing this to me!"

I can't take credit. Dr. Carol Dweck is a researcher at Stanford University and wrote one of my favorite books, *Mindset: The New Psychology of Success.*

In quick summary, the book says that humans can either display a fixed mindset or a growth mindset. Someone with a fixed mindset feels that a label put on them sticks forever, and they identify as that label.

For example, if I were to look at that spectacular failure in the Russian supermarket as an example of how I'll never learn to speak Russian, or never learn to interact with the locals, I would have quit trying and lost out on more years of Russian practice, which I loved, and I would have never created the friendships with people I met after that.

I could have withdrawn, decided never to put myself in that situation again, and only entered situations in which I felt fully comfortable, missing out on some of the best experiences of my life; ultimately, I wouldn't still be living in Spain now.

Throwing myself out there and looking at these "failures" as learning experiences has helped me stay mentally stable through countless cross-cultural blunders.

The trick is to say, "I made a mistake, meaning I don't know how to be successful in that situation **yet**." That "yet" is so powerful. It changes you from labeling yourself a failure to recognizing that you just haven't been able to do it yet. Maybe if I had studied harder, written the word down, or stayed calmer in the situation, it would have changed the outcome.

→» FAST TRACK ACT:
    FIND YOUR GROWTH MINDSET

Starting today, I want you to listen to your inner voice and determine if you currently have more of a fixed mindset or a growth mindset.

If in your inner voice you hear that fixed mindset beating out the growth mindset, talk back to it, and tell it to quiet down so your growth mindset can start to come out.

(I don't recommend talking back to your inner voice out loud—some cultures look down on that.)

You'll know when you have a fixed mindset if you find yourself saying things like, "I'll never be able to do this," "I'm just not good at that," or "I'm a failure or a loser."

Growth mindset is about looking at challenges and failures as learning opportunities. This is perfect for study abroad!

Along the same lines, in all of the work I've done with students and executives, I've seen **five mindset attributes** that all contribute to a successful overseas experience.

- Mindset #1: Ability to See the Positive within the Negative

- Mindset #2: Willingness to Accept Differences and Find Common Ground

- Mindset #3: Tolerance for Ambiguity

- Mindset #4: Willingness to Adapt

- Mindset #5: Motivated by Goals and Prepared for Challenges

Mindset #1: Ability to See the Positive within the Negative

Even when you embarrass yourself with a language mistake, get lost, don't get along with your homestay or roommates, or miss a flight, it's helpful to search for some positive learning experience. I once had a student who got thrown in jail, for a night, when police mistook him for someone else, who had damaged public property. He was scared to death, but he said his Spanish improved so much in those twenty-four hours by speaking with his cellmate! (Very important note: I do NOT recommend going to jail to improve your language skills. Kindly see Chapter 8 for more conventional ways of learning.)

When you train your mind to see the positive side of the inevitable negative, and reframe mistakes as learning opportunities, you prevent yourself from starting a spiral of negativity.

The negatives don't have to be as big as insulting a stranger or getting thrown in jail for a night; even if the airline loses your luggage, on the first day in a new city, that can be a learning opportunity.

Included in this mindset change is a new word that will also change your life: "Probletunity."

At a brilliant conference I attended in Germany, with an American consultant named David Langford, author of *Tool Time for Education*, *Tool Time for Business* and many more, I learned the term he coined called "Probletunity"—a mixture of "problem" and "opportunity." This word has helped me tremendously, shifting my mindset from seeing a problem to seeing an opportunity for improvement.

→ ACT: Here's Your First Chance to Use Probletunity

Step 1: If you are already abroad, think about a "problem" that you have encountered. If you haven't yet arrived, think about a problem back home. Describe what happened. How did you feel? How did you react?

Step 2: How could this problem be transformed into some type of opportunity for you? What actions would you need to take? What is something positive that could come from it?

For example, when I first moved to Barcelona and had no one to hang out with, I didn't just stay in my room and sulk. Well, maybe I did, for a little bit. But then I turned it into the opportunity to discover a new activity that I ended up loving to this day: salsa dancing.

I'll add a slight disclaimer here: I'm not suggesting simply ignoring negative feelings or experiences—quite the opposite. You should be mindful of them, understand them, and embrace them, but ask yourself how they could turn into an opportunity.

Mindset #2: Willingness to Accept Differences and Find Common Ground

I always wanted to be known for some profound statements, but this may be as profound as I get: THINGS WILL BE DIFFERENT. If that's as profound as it gets, that's okay with me, because keeping this one statement in your head will help you adapt to the new culture and develop the intercultural competence we talked about in the last chapter.

A common mistake that people make when crossing cultures is minimizing the differences and saying that "we are all the same deep down; we are all human." It is absolutely true that there are similarities among different cultures, and that is a beautiful thing to discover. However, believing that we are all the same is a dangerous thought that blocks us from accepting that there are differences among people, and those differences are deeply rooted in values and beliefs. It might seem obvious, but it's worth stating: different does NOT mean bad! Study abroad teaches us to appreciate and understand those differences instead of fearing them.

On the surface, yes, across the world you'll see people who drink coffee, eat pizza, meet with friends, and greet each other; but as you'll find out throughout this book, the way that people do those things, and the values behind those behaviors, may be completely different.

Someone who is not willing to accept differences blinds themselves to the ability to iceberg. And when someone can't iceberg, they will not be able to see things from a different perspective.

On the flip side, accepting these differences helps us to adapt. When you see things as new and possibly annoying, just remember, you have gone abroad to experience what will be different, and sometimes that difference is frustrating and challenging.

Even now, when I get frustrated by something different in the culture where I'm traveling, I take a deep breath, and I say, "Things will be different." I accept that, and it relaxes me. Try it out in whatever country you are in!

At the same time, students who are most successful are the ones **who can also find common ground across cultures**. Seeking out the differences isn't meant to create a divide of "us" versus "them." The idea behind iceberging is to understand the fascinating different ways in which people see the world, but also to find the commonalities between cultures. This creates connections because we understand each other better.

Some similarities can only be appreciated by diving much deeper down. For example, I've been with students as they drank traditional mint tea with Moroccan families living vastly different lives than their own, in distant mountain villages; but they connected on a deep level when they discovered that seemingly opposite behaviors and beliefs were driven by common values like love for their family. Whereas American individualism might say the best way for a teenager to learn is to go out on their own, make mistakes, and learn for themselves, this family suggested that the best way for young people to learn life skills is from their close-knit extended family, not needing to venture far from home. Although it sounds somewhat paradoxical, identifying commonalities and, simultaneously, appreciating the differences among cultures are two essential skills, not just while abroad but also for everyday life.

Mindset #3: Tolerance for Ambiguity

Ambiguity means that something can be interpreted in various ways and we are not certain what will happen next. When we are swimming in our own cultural waters, we can often predict how someone will react to our behavior. We can anticipate what they are going to do or say, or the way they will behave in response to us.

However, when we go to other cultures, where the rules have changed, all of that gets flipped on its head, and we find ourselves in situations that are like some strange alternate universe where people are not reacting the way we expect.

People who are successful while living overseas learn to tolerate that ambiguity.

Mindset #4: Willingness to Adapt

Once you've gained an awareness of the differences in the culture and understand more about your own culture and identity, you have to be willing to bridge that gap and adapt. Like the chapter of this title tells us, and like my boss drilled into me, you have to adapt to the culture; the culture won't adapt to you.

Take an example of punctuality. Imagine if a student from a culture where it is normal to arrive to class several minutes late goes to study in the US and always arrives five minutes after the class starts. It's unlikely that the professor will laugh it off, accept it, and say, "Let's change the way that we do things to adapt to this person." That student will have to adapt or will end up suffering.

Mindset #5: Motivated by Goals and Prepared for Challenges

Let's start with the goals. If you've done the activity, in Chapter 1, about setting your SMART goals, you are on your way!

As we've seen, there will also be loads of challenges during your time abroad, which is great, because they will help you grow the most. Earlier,

I mentioned the "study abroad magic." There's a saying: *all magic has a price*. These challenges will be the currency with which you purchase that study abroad magic, and it will be well worth the cost.

One way to prepare for those challenges is to be motivated to step out of your comfort zone.

I have seen the awesome impact of this, in my own experiences and in working with thousands of students abroad. Many people say that outside of your comfort zone is where the magic happens.

Are you ready to take that step? You could have just stayed home and done another semester or summer school, at your university, or accepted an internship in your hometown. But you decided that you wanted more. More is waiting for you, but you have to seek it out.

→ ACT: Comfort-Zone Challenge

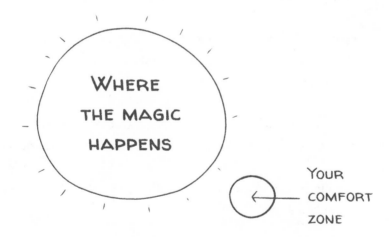

Here are some ideas for you to step out of your comfort zone. I'd like to put them in order of easiest to hardest, but that depends on every person individually, so you will have to be the one to decide how far you can go. The best part is that something that seems hard, right now, will seem easier in the future (if you are pushing yourself).

As you psych yourself up for these, this advice from a personal-coach friend of mine might help: sometimes we have to take a short-term hit to happiness to eventually grow even more later.

So the assignment is easy: do one of these challenges, and write down how it makes you feel. Write as much as you can about the experience. Even if you are not abroad yet, some of these will still work for you. Just make sure you go out and try them when you get to your new city too.

- Go explore a new part of town by yourself.

- Go explore a new part of town by yourself, and only use a paper map, not Google Maps.

- If you are used to getting around your city on one type of transportation, take a different type. For example, if you only use the metro, tube, or subway, then take a bus.

- If you usually walk from your home to your school or internship, take a different route every day, for a week—even if it takes you more time.

- Start talking to a stranger (but safely). Strike up a conversation with someone who works at a café or restaurant that you frequent.

- If you love your social media, go without social media for twenty-four hours.

By changing your mindset, to see the positive, and being willing to push yourself out of your comfort zone, you have made huge progress towards gaining some of the magic of study abroad growth.

DIVE DEEPER INTO...

→ Growth mindset vs. fixed mindset:

Carol S. Dweck, *Mindset: The New Psychology of Success* (New York City: Random House, 2006).

Carol S. Dweck, "The Power of Believing That You Can Improve," Ted. com, video 10:11, December 17, 2014, https://www.ted.com/talks/carol_dweck_the_power_of_believing_that_you_can_improve?language=en.

→ Developmental model of intercultural sensitivity:

"Developmental Mental Model of Intercultural Sensitivity," Organizing Engagement, accessed January 15, 2022, https://organizingengagement. org/models/developmental-model-of-intercultural-sensitivity/.

Chapter 4

DISCOVERING YOURSELF ALONG THE WAY

MAKING PANCAKES

One morning, when I was first living with my girlfriend Kerry (who is now my wife and, you will remember, is from England), I had a hankering for pancakes. I had maple syrup, but I complained that I couldn't find the box of pancake mix any-where, so I was going to head out to this store called "The Taste of Home," which is the place where we expats go to splurge on all of the comfort foods that we "need," like marshmallows, canned soup, instant gravy, and Rice-A-Roni in a box. (MUCH more on iceberging all of that in Chapter 11). When I said this to Kerry, she couldn't believe it and looked at me like I was crazy. She said, "You realize that making pancakes is the easiest thing in the world? Do you have flour? Do you have eggs? Do you have butter? Do you have WATER?! Then you can make pancakes. You don't need a box."

How's that for in-your-face culture shock? In that moment of getting berated, I realized how much I valued, and relied on, convenience. I was so used to the convenience of "just add water" that I never, in my years, had stopped to think about it.

ICEBERG YOURSELF!

Before we go much deeper into learning about the other cultures, we're going to start with *you*, because we must get to know ourselves before we can understand other cultures—also, because you know yourself best, although I'm willing to bet not as well as you think. This chapter is like a mini cultural and identity self-assessment.

These activities will help you do something that sounds painful—we are going to iceberg ourselves!

When we travel abroad, we learn as much about ourselves, and our own culture, as we do about the people and the new culture we are visit-ing/experiencing for the first time.

Why? Because cultural incidents happen all of the time. Sometimes they are in our face, like someone from another culture making fun of us for making out-of-the-box pancakes (ironically one of the least "out of the box" ways of cooking); or a subtle thought in our heads wondering, *Why are they doing that?*; and can range to an extremely visceral physical experience that makes us feel threatened, annoyed, confused, etc.

These cultural incidents help us to stop and ask two wonderfully powerful questions:

QUESTIONS

1. Why do they do that?

2. Why do I do what I do?

Luckily, we have our faithful iceberg to help us out in exactly these situations.

The iceberg helps us learn about our identities because there are many explicit aspects of our identities, above the water, but there are also parts hidden, or even mistaken, below the water.

OUR IDENTITIES AND CULTURE INTERTWINED

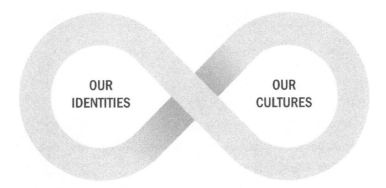

What do we learn about ourselves as individuals, while abroad, and how does that fit into national identities or culture?

We've been talking a lot about national cultures, but sometimes we don't identify wholly with our culture's tendencies, because each one of us is an individual and, therefore, doesn't fit into a nice, neat, prepackaged description. You might find yourself saying that a cultural tendency, even one demonstrated to be true for most Americans, doesn't describe you. Of course! That's because we have to look both at the cultural tendencies of a group of people and at ourselves as individuals.

→》 FAST TRACK ACT: YOUR SIXTH SENSE × 3

One of my favorite—and most effective—activities to do with students is Your Sixth Sense × 3, where the goal is to write three lists of six adjectives describing cultures. Easy, right? Actually, there is much more to this deceptively simple activity, so don't start writing until you've read the descriptions. Let's do a deep dive on each of the following steps, and you can write your lists as we dive. You're going to:

Step 1: Write down six adjectives that describe your home culture.

Step 2: Write down six adjectives that describe the culture where you are studying.

Step 3: Write down six adjectives that people from the culture where you are studying would use to describe your culture.

STEP 1:

Write down six adjectives to describe your home culture.

Remember, an adjective describes a word, so don't write down verbs or nouns, but a description.

For example, imagine you are on a plane flying from abroad back to the US, and you're sitting next to a citizen of that other country; that person turns to you and says, "I have never been to your country before, and I don't really know much about it. Tell me what the culture is like. What are people like?"

And then pretend, for some strange reason, that you only speak in one-word sentences using adjectives. What would you say to that person?

Give yourself a few minutes to write down six adjectives.

How did you do? Did you come up with six?

If you didn't, that's ok; don't feel bad. Most students who haven't lived outside of their home country can't come up with six. Why? It's back to our friend the fish. If you have been mostly swimming in your own waters, it's really hard to know what your waters are like. Until you are confronted with different ways of doing things and seeing the world, and you learn to reflect on those differences, it's hard to put into words the way you do it. I didn't understand my deep need for convenience or punctuality, until I was confronted with the opposite, because that's what I had always known. I thought *everyone values those things, too,* so why would I even point it out?

Hold on to your answers for now, as we move on to Step 2.

STEP 2:

Write down six adjectives that describe the culture where you are studying. What are people like there?

Stop now and take a few minutes to do this.

Now think to yourself, where did your answers come from? Have you already lived in that country or traveled there for vacation? Do you know several people, personally, who are from that country? Or do your ideas come from TV shows, movies, or from someone you know, who has been there before and told you their opinions?

With the thousands of students I have worked with doing this activity the answer is most frequently: I have never been to that country before, and I don't really know anyone from there, so I guess these ideas come from others, who have told me their opinions, or from what I have learned in classes and what I've seen in movies.

What do we call it when we make a judgment about a group of people when we don't know much about them?

Yes, a stereotype!

It is normal, as a human being, to try to make sense out of something we don't fully understand, and so we generalize and compartmentalize; that's what our brains do automatically. However, stereotypes are hurtful and damaging when we hold on to those ignorant ideas of "the other" even when we get new information telling us the opposite. Generalizations allow for individual differences instead of labels that are meant to stick to every member of a group.

For example, suppose someone was coming to the US but had never actually met an American or been there before, only watched lots of TV and read the headlines of US newspapers; their six adjectives describing American culture might be:

- Wealthy
- Fit (as in physically fit)
- Consumeristic
- Friendly
- Gun-toting
- Politically active

If, upon arriving in the US, they met an American who didn't own a gun, then one who didn't have much money, and another who didn't appear to be athletic or friendly, and, instead of adjusting their perception, simply considered each of them the exception, that would be a problem. Stereotypes are dangerous when we are unwilling to change them. This is why it's so important to write down what we think we know about a culture, carefully observe and interact with it as much as possible, and then iceberg our findings, modifying any generalizations along the way. Only then can we more confidently start to understand their culture and back away from stereotypes.

Be Aware of Confirmation Bias

We humans are all guilty of confirmation bias. This means that we have certain stereotypes in our heads, and we seek out evidence to confirm that stereotype or judgment and dismiss anything that doesn't fit it. The great thing about Step 2 of this activity is that it lays bare what might be your confirmation bias, so you can try to avoid it. Just make sure you are actively looking for those exceptions, not just seeking out the examples that confirm your initial label.

STEP 3:

Write down six adjectives that people from the culture where you are studying would use to describe your culture.

So, for example, if you are an American going to Japan, how do you think Japanese people would describe Americans?

This step is important because it helps you know what you are getting into. When we meet new people, we never start with a blank slate, without bias. At first glance, people are making judgments about us. The same goes for our culture. People around the world already have a judgment about *us* because of what they think of our *countries*.

If those six adjectives you wrote down for this step do not describe you personally, then you will have to work a little harder to overcome the false perception of who they think you are.

This ACT that you have just finished will never really end. Throughout the rest of your time abroad, and I would say throughout the rest of your life, you will constantly be confronted with situations where your mind categorizes a certain culture, or a person, without first gathering much information. And others will do the same about you—as an individual and as someone who belongs to your culture(s). My challenge to you is to keep this Your Sixth Sense × 3 activity in mind and try to gather the all-around perspective, before jumping to conclusions. Imagine how much kinder the world could be if everyone did this.

OUR CULTURAL LENS

Why do we always start by describing our own culture in that last activity? I hope you are sitting down because this is about to get deep. To quote the author Anaïs Nin, "We don't see things as they are, we see them as we are."

Boom. Damn that's profound, and I love it. I wish that had been my quote. It's so good it bears repeating: "We don't see things as they are, we see them as we are."

So often, during this Your Sixth Sense × 3 activity, we find that the way we describe the other culture is the opposite of how we've described ourselves. For example, with my American students coming to Spain:

Step 1: Americans are fast-paced.

Step 2: Spaniards are laid-back.

Step 1: Americans are punctual.

Step 2: Spaniards are not punctual.

This is our "cultural lens." When we look at something in another culture and see it as rude, strange, fast-paced, laid-back, or some similar judgment call, *we have to look back at ourselves to see why we see it that way.* We are comparing them to the way we are.

Remember this wonderful pair of questions:

1. Why do they do that?

2. Why do I do what I do?

→ Where Does Our Cultural Lens Come From?

Our cultural lens is impacted by family, nationality, friends, history, religion, gender, beliefs, values, prejudices, experiences, fears, and feelings.

When I judged my host mom to be rude when she just said *"ponme un café con leche"* instead of saying it the "polite way"—"I would like a coffee with milk please."—I was judging her through my cultural lens.

What's happening here is that *two people can look at the exact same thing but interpret it very differently.*

REAL-WORLD EXAMPLES OF TWO PEOPLE INTERPRETING DIFFERENTLY

I was out having some tapas with some of my new Spanish friends in Madrid while studying abroad. Tapas are small plates of food that people share, often for snacks or light meals. The thing to do is *tapear*, which is to bounce from place to place, enjoying one specialty, at this small bar, and then on to the next one.

That night, we walked past a bar specializing in grilled garlic shrimp, and my friend said, "Let's go in here." I took one look and blurted out my initial reaction: "But it's so dirty in there. Really? That's where you want to go?"

My "dirty" came from the fact that there were greasy, messy, used napkins all over the floor, that people were standing on. My friends looked at me like I was crazy and said, "It's *because* of all of the napkins on the floor that we want to go in there."

As we were using our hands to eat our delicious, super-garlicky shrimp, that are stacked four-high, covered in olive oil, all on a small piece of bread and held in place with a toothpick, they explained to me: in that bar, the tapas are oily and greasy, and you use a lot of napkins. The waiters are so busy carrying food around that, if they had to touch our dirty, germ-ridden napkins and keep washing their hands all the time, they couldn't get the food to people quickly enough, and it would be pretty disgusting. Instead, people throw their napkins on the floor, and every ten minutes or so, one of the workers comes around with a broom and, in seconds, sweeps the floor clean, just for it to be filled again soon...if it's a good place. That's the key, and that's what my friends were saying: the fact that it had so many napkins on the floor meant that it's popular and it's good.

It made total sense to me after they explained it! Note that not all Spaniards feel the same about the napkins on the floor. Some of my Spanish friends are totally against it. Once again, two people can look at the same thing and see it very differently.

A very basic example would be when a student of mine, whose family was from India, ate "spicy" food that tasted bland to her, but another student, who was not used to spice, felt like her mouth was on fire. These examples are simplistic, but they show that where we come from and what we are used to affects how we experience and interpret.

Who is right and who is wrong, in these examples? The answer is, and this is important: **most of the time** there is not a universal right or wrong; there is only what is right and wrong *in that cultural context,* which is the fun—and the hard—part when you are trying to figure it all out.

The important question for your personal and professional growth is: can you learn to see things from the other perspective even if you don't agree with it?

To underscore this point, when we grasp that two people can look at the same thing and interpret it differently, it helps us adapt. It also reinforces the idea that we need to suspend judgment, because it's often hard to see something from another perspective when we have seen it one way for so long. If I didn't have those friends explain it to me, and then actually experience it myself in the "dirty/popular" bar, I would have gone on with the judgment solely from my cultural lens.

So the next time you find yourself using the words "normal," "rude," or "wrong," think about your cultural lens and where those judgments are coming from. They come from your culture and your identity.

ICEBERG AND IDENTITIES: MISTAKEN AND HIDDEN IDENTITIES

IDENTITIES

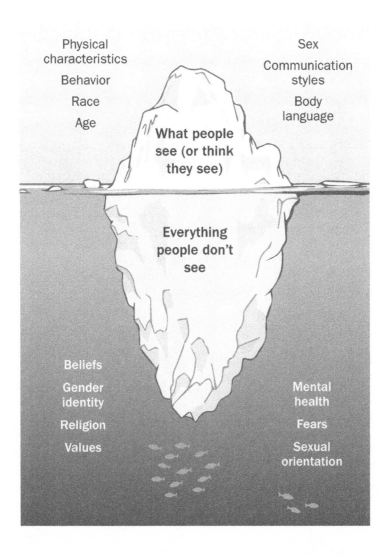

→ ACT: How Do You Respond to This Query: "Tell Me about Yourself."

Imagine I meet you for the first time, and I say, "Tell me about yourself." How do you answer? In many ways, it's difficult: How do you briefly define yourself? How does it change in different contexts? Which aspects of your identity do you choose to talk about? Think about your values, beliefs, and what you care about. What is the story that led you to arrive where you are?

Take a few minutes to write down how you would answer that question.

The answer to that question gets to the heart of our identity or, better yet, identities. Our identities get formed much like our cultural lens does, through the relationships that we have to the people around us and by:

- Religion
- Family
- Heritage
- Ethnicity
- Race
- Sexual orientation
- Gender identity
- Sports clubs you belong to
- Age

Maybe you've answered: I'm a young American woman, a student at X university studying premed, I have a younger brother, I play volleyball, I work at a local retail store on the weekends, and I have a dog named Fluffy that I spoil silly.

You've said some layers of your identity here include:

- Young
- American
- Woman

- Student
- Premed student
- Sibling
- Athlete
- Worker
- Dog owner

What happens when you go abroad? These identities often get shifted, put on pause, or rethought, and you discover new ones. You may even have one identity at home and another abroad. One reason this happens is that people from other cultures may interact with your identities differently than what you are used to.

With this example above, the student may study abroad in England, for a semester, take an Entrepreneurship class, and decide she wants to start her own business and drop premed to switch majors. And maybe she can't find anywhere to play volleyball, or any gyms she wants to go to, and feels she is losing her "athlete" identity; and she can't work, while abroad, so doesn't have the "worker" identity anymore; and she will miss pampering her dog. Her feelings about what it means to be an American may also shift when looking at the US from other countries' perspectives. Finally, she may find that what it means to be young, or a woman, shifts in the new cultural context.

→ Identities Lost, Found, and Rewound

Don't underestimate how difficult this loss or change of identity is! Think about that fish in the water, swimming around on cultural autopilot; we humans are like that too. It's a shock to the system, when our environment changes, because we have to adapt, and we inevitably change, too.

I am a White, straight, middle-class, cisgender male who has grown up with immense privileges, compared to many people around the world, and I certainly experienced these changes.

I cannot speak firsthand to other students' identities that I don't possess. However, I want and need to address them in this book; but I recognize that my own background wouldn't let me do it justice, and it would take volumes to do so. My goal is to give you some tools and food for thought to reflect on your identities, in new ways, and then point you to more in-depth resources.

→ Nontraditional Identity

I want to give a special shout-out here to the nontraditional students whose identities and roles may shift significantly when they go abroad. When we say nontraditional, we are talking about a student who isn't the statistically typical eighteen to twenty-one-year-old going to a four-year college or university. Many nontraditional students study abroad and may have even more identities that are harder to shed, like spouse, parent, full-time worker, live-in caretaker, or someone working two jobs, going to school, and taking care of a family. Even though they don't stop being a spouse or a parent, when they go abroad, the dynamic shifts, completely, from being on call 24/7 to being an ocean away.

→ Mistaken Identity

I had a Mexican-American student in Spain—let's call him Pablo Garcia— who struggled because, although he has a Hispanic name and looks like he should speak Spanish, he didn't speak well at all, mostly *Spanglish*, and Spanish at a basic level. His parents wanted him to learn English in the US, so that's the language they used at home. People he met abroad immediately made assumptions about him that were entirely wrong. He got exhausted explaining his background story to people over and over.

He also explained that he is a different person when he speaks Spanish. His identity shifts, even back home. He said it's because they are different cultures, different ways of acting to fit in.

BIPOC (Black, Indigenous, and people of color) students I've worked with, over the years, have told me about similar experiences of mistaken or changed identities. One Black student, who wore a do-rag, said that every conversation he had with someone new ended up with him explaining what a do-rag is, why he wears it, and why it doesn't mean he is a rapper, a hooligan, or any of the other stereotypes associated with it. He told me do-rags are used to protect hairstyles, braids, and waves, for sun protection, or worn when working out. While, in a way, he was happy to set people straight and clear up negative stereotypes, by the end, it was so tiring he just couldn't have the conversation anymore.

Another student, who is Indian-American, told me that she was referred to as "exotic," in different countries across Europe, and did not know whether to take it as a compliment or an insult.

"I don't necessarily take offense to it, but calling someone 'exotic' as a compliment—in my opinion—implies that they're 'different,' and when I think about the word, it just reminds me of an exotic parrot or plant. I don't mind being different, but when people emphasize it, while trying to touch my hair and flirt with me, for example, I do find it a bit uncomfortable. At the end of the day, though, I don't think the people who say this to me are being malicious."
—Nadia J.

→ ACT: Changed Identities

Step 1: Write down all of the identities you have, at home, that may be changed, put on pause, or shift significantly because of the context while you are abroad. For example, I'm a dad, and if I went to study abroad again, without my kids, I wouldn't stop being a dad, but my role as a dad would have changed greatly.

Here are some types of identity to think about:
- cultural identity
- professional identity
- ethnic and national identity
- religious identity
- gender identity
- disability identity

Step 2: Now, write down how you feel about those identities changing. These don't all have to be difficult. Maybe you are looking forward to not having to work a nighttime job, be president of your fraternity, or wake up at 5:30 a.m. to work out for volleyball.

→ Hidden Identity

We can think about identity like an onion with many layers; only some are visible, until you peel down deeper.

Depending on how we dress, walk, talk, and act, people make assumptions about our identities. Are we shy? Do we have money? Do we fit in with the crowds? Are we more individual and stick out? Do we adhere to the gender norms of society? Do we make an effort to care about our appearance? What is our skin color, and what does that mean in that cultural context? Unfortunately, they are making assumptions based on what's above the water without getting to know the true identity below the water.

A hidden identity could have to do with sexual orientation, gender identity, race, religious affiliation, mental health, family history—any aspect of who we are that can't be known just by looking at us.

All of this might make you think *these people don't know the real me!* That discrepancy between who you are and how others see you can be truly jarring if you are not prepared.

→ Coming Out Abroad

One friend I spoke to mentioned how many students today coming from more liberal areas of the US never have to "come out" like past generations. From an early age, it is known and accepted that someone doesn't fit the sexual-orientation norms of the past, so there is not a surprising "coming out" talk. That makes it even more shocking if they go to a more conservative country and find that they do have to "come out"—either to the host family, local friends, or other students on the program.

The opposite could also be true. Maybe the student comes from a place in the US where being LGTBQ was shunned, or they didn't have a support group at home, yet when they go abroad, they find that the culture is more supportive. They may meet other students, or locals, who live openly and confidently as members of the LGBTQ community, which bolsters their own courage. Their identity as LGBTQ hasn't changed, but their fortitude and attitude to be comfortable being who they are has changed.

Connecting with the LGBTQ community, where you are studying, could be an excellent way to meet new people and learn more about the culture. Since some cultures may be less tolerant, it's best to make sure you understand that society's attitude towards the LGBTQ community, in case safety is an issue.

→ ACT: Your Identity Iceberged

Step 1: Just by looking at you, what will people observe about you? Write down all that you can.

For example:

- They will see I am a college student.
- They will see I am not from here (here being the place where you are studying).
- They will see I am tall.
- They will see my arms covered in tattoos.

.ep 2: What might people ASSUME they know about you by what they can see? Take some time to write this down.

Step 3: What are your hidden identities that people can't determine by just looking at you? Finish this sentence: *just by looking at me, people won't be able to tell that I am…* For example: gay, very religious, a first-generation student, an amazing singer, a person who suffers from depression, etc.

PREPARING TO BE A FISH OUT OF WATER

This testing of our identities is frustrating. When we are abroad, we are more likely to have people "call us out" because of our identity. For example, they might say that's "just like an American to [fill in the blank with a stereotype]."

When abroad, students become much more philosophical about who they are. With this constant testing and questioning of why things are going "wrong,"—meaning different from what they expected—they start to question:

- What is going on?
- What is wrong with me?
- How and where do I fit in?

The good news is that nothing is wrong with you, and the better news is that all of this questioning is the growth process we go through to help us know ourselves better and feel more comfortable and confident in who we are; we are discovering ourselves along the way. That confidence will serve you well, later in life, so treasure those moments of discomfort and ambiguity (when possible) and reflect on them with these activities.

While our identities are individual, they also help us connect to others who similarly identify. Reflecting on those connections prepares us for what we might experience in the new cultural context.

Christina Thompson, Founder of Compear Global Education Network Consulting and Director of Diversity Outreach for Barcelona Study Abroad Experience, poses these questions to Black students to prepare them to think about Black Identity Abroad:

→ Before

How are you preparing yourself for your travels? Do you have any expectations?

While you are abroad, how will you connect with Black people with different cultural backgrounds?

How do you think being Black will affect your experience abroad?

→ While Abroad

Were there any moments where you had to educate people on Black culture?

Were there any moments you felt you experienced prejudice? How did you manage it?

→ After Returning Home

Did you find that Black culture manifested itself differently abroad?

Do you think your own sense of Black culture was challenged? If so, in what ways?

→ ACT: Your Identity Abroad

Take these questions above, about Black identity, and answer them for yourself, replacing "Black Identity" with a particular aspect of your identity that you want to focus on. You might replace it with American, Jewish, LGBTQ, Muslim, mobility-challenged, hearing-impaired, blond-haired, light-skinned, etc.

→ ACT: Spend Time Alone

It's time to get philosophical and spend some time thinking about your identity. That's hard to do when you are constantly with other people or connected to technology. So this activity asks you to spend some time alone—not connected to any electronics. Use that time to answer some of the questions above or walk around and get to know the city—visit a park, or a forest, or wherever, but do it alone with your own thoughts. In fact, leave your phone at home! Notice the difference in how much you pay attention to everything around you (and in your head) when you don't even have the option of getting on your phone.

DON'T SAY THAT ABOUT MY CULTURE!

Like that fish in water, when we are surrounded by people who think and act like we do, we don't often have to question how we do things. But by taking the leap out of the water and experiencing different perspectives, we learn so much about ourselves.

When that happens, we tend to get defensive about "our way" because we've always known it as the best way. This can lead to ethnocentrism, which is when we go to the extreme, thinking that our culture is "the model" or "the example" and everything else revolves around our culture. Like someone who is egocentric and thinks everything revolves around them, ethnocentrism is the same, but at a cultural and country level.

It's hard when people criticize your culture or identity, but I challenge you not to jump to any conclusions and get too defensive yet. Know that your first reaction might be a desire to suggest that your way is the right way but challenge yourself to see it from the other perspective first. Later you can interpret, evaluate, and make stronger arguments.

Going back to the PDA example—if you find yourself defending how "right it is" for a couple to get a room, when they are kissing, and how "wrong it is" to make out in public, try to see it from the other perspective. Make sure you iceberg it on both sides to see the values behind those behaviors, then try to reconcile them with your own before getting too defensive.

BUILDING A NETWORK OF SUPPORT

Even if you are looking forward to temporarily losing some of these identities, it can still take a while to adjust, and it's best to have a network of support to help you get through it.

What will you do to build this network while abroad? Will it be part of your program, or something you have to do on your own, like joining a sports team, a religious organization, or a club or even volunteering at the local dog shelter so you get your fix of canine interaction? Whatever it is, this network is not just a great way for you to find support but also a brilliant way to reach many of the goals we talk about in this book.

ICC PART II—YOUR OWN VALUES AND BELIEFS

In the last chapter, we began talking about Intercultural Competence (ICC), one of the strongest traits of global leaders. We defined it as: the ability to understand the values and beliefs behind behavior (*we saw how to do this with the iceberg*) and reconcile them with your own (values and beliefs).

Now that you have iceberged yourself, you've started to work on that second part: "and reconcile them with your own." This is a deeper way to discover yourself along the way.

The great challenge and fun, now, is to keep working hard, to understand the values and beliefs behind the behaviors of different cultures, and force yourself to think about how *your values and beliefs* can fit with them.

Mastering that will be a lifelong lesson, which help you, tremendously, to work effectively with other cultures.

DIVE DEEPER INTO...

→ Diversity abroad:

"Articles: Helpful Resources to Help You Prepare Abroad," Diversity Abroad, accessed January 15, 2022, https://www.diversityabroad.com/articles.

→ Diversity and identity abroad:

Anu Taranath, *Beyond Guilt Trips: Mindful Travel in an Unequal World* (Toronto: Between the Lines, 2019).

"Diversity & Identity Abroad," University of Colorado Boulder, accessed January 15, 2022, https://abroad.colorado.edu/index.cfm?FuseAction=Abroad.ViewLink&Parent_ID=0&Link_ID=6E204190-009B-E1E0-D27FB8091127949E.

Adriana Smith, *Studying Abroad for Black Women (Diary of a Traveling Black Woman: A Guide to International Travel)* (Atlanta: Travelling Black Women, Grace Royal International, LLC, 2019).

→ Strategies to overcome difficulties in changed identities across cultures:

Andy Molinsky, *Global Dexterity: How to Adapt Your Behavior across Cultures without Losing Yourself in the Process* (Boston: Harvard Business Review Press, 2013).

Chapter 5

THE PRICE OF MAGIC

There's no doubt about it: this study abroad adventure could be very hard at times. Is it worth the money, time, effort, and investment you put into it? YES! Absolutely.

The benefits are immense and long-lasting, even in a short study abroad experience.

Study abroad is a High Impact Practice (HIP)—meaning it brings huge opportunities for growth during an intense period. And the beauty is that these are not skills that are only useful while you are in another country; these are transferable skills, useful in every other aspect of your life. The effort you put into it should pay off tremendously, both for living a happier, less regretful life and for job satisfaction and financial success.

Before we look into how you can reap all of those benefits, let's see why this experience, which looks like a honeymoon in our friends' social media and the study abroad catalogs, is, in reality, so challenging.

ALL THAT'S NEW

Here is just a short list of the things that are new when we study abroad:

- New foods
- New "mom"
- New culture
- New friends
- New language
- New identities
- New surroundings
- New transportation
- New personal space
- New way of walking
- New schedules
- New smells
- New way of communicating

- New "right" or "wrong"
- New "rude" or "polite"
- New way of studying
- New way of working
- New gender relations
- New prejudices

All of that "newness" makes the situation ripe for mistake after mistake and frustration after frustration. But don't despair! And don't change your mind about study abroad.

You will soon learn to *seek out* that newness, no matter how hard or uncomfortable it is at first, because you realize all you can gain from experiencing it.

TRANSFERABLE SKILLS BORN AND BOOSTED

I have listed, below, Cultural Superpowers that can be acquired and strengthened through engaged study abroad. This is a list of important skills that employers are looking for. My list comes from several places, including Forbes Coaching Council (an invitation-only organization for senior-level executives in the coaching industry), alumni surveys, multiple career and cross-cultural books, and my own experience as a business owner.

Originally, I was going to create two lists:

1. Skills to become more employable and a better employee

2. Skills to live a happier life

But the more I worked on this, the more I realized that these two lists go hand in hand. When you become more adaptable to unfamiliar situations, an employer will love that trait, because they can send you into all kinds of new situations and you will thrive. That's a benefit for the employer. At the same time, when you go into those new situations with confidence and less stress, because you are adaptable and know you can learn something from it (even if you fail), you are a happier person.

I've said it before, and I'll say it again: what other experience can you have, in such a short period, that will give you all of this?!

THE CULTURAL SUPERPOWERS LIST

I've whittled this list down to just a "Top 10" out of the dozens that could go in here. Throughout the book, you'll see activities to help you build these skills. These superpowers are in no particular order. To me, they are all equally important.

→ 1. Adaptability

You have the ability to be more spontaneous; to not fear a change of plans or a situation that is completely unknown or ambiguous; to face unfamiliar situations and accept change with a sense of humor.

→ 2. Empathy

The skill to see things from someone else's perspective and understand their values and why they feel the way they do. When you can do this, you can work better with others and effectively in a team.

→ 3. Resilience

You're able to bounce back and carry on after difficult life events. You can withstand adversity.

→ 4. Perseverance

Specifically, the ability to view failure as a way to learn something new. You'll see your failures as growth opportunities instead of as something to bring you down or as a label that sticks.

→ 5. Sense of Humor

This is especially valuable in difficult situations. The book *Humor, Seriously,* by Jennifer Aaker and Naomi Bagdonas demonstrates how bosses and colleagues are rated higher when they can introduce some type of levity or humor into a situation.

→ 6. Self-Awareness

You'll become much more aware of your own values and beliefs. This develops the all-important skill of knowing your sense of purpose, as well as your strengths and weaknesses.

→ 7. Communication

Not only can you learn to speak other languages and have the ability to work and make friends with people from around the world, but you'll also develop active listening and active watching (nonverbal communication) skills.

→ 8. Curiosity

This includes a thirst for knowledge. The aha and lightbulb moments abroad are so powerful and addictive that you will soon seek out more and more of them. This curiosity and search for knowledge is something that most employers highly value and that comes in handy if you are an entrepreneur.

→ 9. Confidence

When you realize that you can make it through the big and small challenges abroad, you feel the strength to overcome anything that life throws at you.

→ 10. Optimism

You'll train yourself to have a positive outlook on life. Studies show that optimistic people are twice as likely to be successful, less likely to divorce, etc.

Gaining those cultural superpowers is a lot to promise, I know. How can I (and the entire field of international education) be so confident that these transformations happen?

Let me start with one specific, powerful story.

~~~~~~

SCOTT'S STORY

Here is a beautiful story about transformation from study abroad with one of my former students. During one summer when I led a group of high-school students to Spain, I had one student, Scott, who was sixteen years old. When we started the trip in Madrid, an extremely nervous Scott said to me, "I am a very dependent person and can't do much on my own, so will you stay with me?" He didn't have to tell me that, because I knew it; he didn't leave my side.

When the other students, who weren't much older than he was, had free time, they would go off and explore, but Scott did whatever I did, so he didn't have to be without me. We spent the first couple of days like that until he finally felt comfortable enough to go off with the rest of the group somewhere for short periods.

But when we arrived in Granada—a city in the south of Spain where we lived with families and where the students attended Spanish classes—we went back to the same routine, and Scott mostly became my shadow again while slowly, day-by-day, gaining more independence. On the first day of class, his host family took him to the school, on the city bus, and by day two or three, he soon felt comfortable enough to do that on his own. For any activities that we had planned, that first week, in different parts of the city, either his host family or I would accompany him, while other students could make their way there on their own.

In the second week, Scott experienced an adventure that dramatically pulled him out of his comfort zone. One night he had to take a taxi, by himself, to meet the group in an unfamiliar area of Granada, after hoping to have me come pick him up, something I couldn't manage logistically. As frightening and new as it was, he felt a sense of accomplishment by overcoming that challenge, which gave him more courage and confidence for what was still to come.

Lo and behold, by the third week, Scott found his way everywhere independently in Granada.

I was worried, though, when we made it back to Madrid, a city ten times the size of Granada. At the hotel, I handed out maps (paper maps, not Google Maps; this was 1999) and gave instructions to meet at a restaurant about a fifteen-minute walk from where we were. The other students told Scott where they were going and asked him if he wanted to join them. When he said no, I instinctively asked him if he wanted to walk around with me for a while. That's when he almost brought me to tears. He said, "No, I just want to go explore by myself. I can do this."

In five weeks, step-by-step, he had become so much more independent and confident. I remember hearing from his parents that they couldn't believe the impact that summer had on his trajectory to adulthood.

I had the extreme pleasure of getting back in touch with Scott, all these years later, and sharing this story with him. Here is his response:

> Even twenty-three years later, I was just thinking about this experience the other day. Our trip to Spain, back in 1999, really was a moment of so many firsts for me. First time out of the United States. First time away from my parents and family for any extended period of time. First time ever taking public transport, whether it was a bus or metro train (never mind by myself). First time taking a taxi.
>
> I may have really struggled connecting with people and not realized exactly what I was doing, at the time, but my experiences of being introduced to new environments and people ultimately planted the seeds years later to help me to continue to reflect and discover, better interact with new people

(even in other languages), form better working relationships, and yes, even help form new friendships. For that, I am forever proud and grateful.

—Scott Rich

~~~~~~

As this story shows us, building these cultural superpowers takes time. You don't wake up one morning and say: "Look at that—I'm adaptable!" or, "Now I can empathize!" The growth happens by working through the challenges and progressing over time.

I could give you story after story of similar transformations, but let's look into some of the reasons why this happens when you study abroad.

CREATING KNOWLEDGE THROUGH EXPERIENCE

Dr. David Kolb is a brilliant philosopher, educator, and author, renowned for his work on experiential learning. His findings help us understand why study abroad has so much potential for personal and professional growth.

"Learning is the process whereby knowledge is created through the transformation of experience." (Kolb, 1984, p. 38)

Kolb's Experiential Learning Cycle contains four stages, which I will simplify here, but I encourage you to learn more with the resource in the *Dive Deeper Into…* section below:

→ 1. Concrete **Experience**

This is especially powerful when it is a new experience or situation, or it could be a new way of interpreting an experience you've had before.

Study abroad provides ample opportunity for new experiences and to reinterpret experiences, such as a new way to buy food, trying to decipher a new style of communication, or new way to get from point A to point B.

→ 2. **Reflective** Observation

In this stage, the learner should reflect on that new experience and consider any inconsistencies between the experience and their understanding.

That's what this book helps you do! The activities are designed to build in this reflection, so you will compare your values and beliefs with the new ones you encounter.

→ 3. Abstract **Thinking**

Here, your reflection creates a change in an existing abstract concept that you previously held, a new way of absorbing an idea.

When we dive under the water and try to understand why others do what they do, and why we do what we do, this deeper understanding makes the learning stick.

→ 4. Active **Experimentation**

You now take these new ideas and start to apply them to your new surroundings to see what happens.

As you live in your new cultural waters, apply the new knowledge you have gained about unique cultural rules; you make mistakes, try again, over and over—that is your active experimentation.

The magic is that you can encounter new experiences, all the time, and it starts the cycle all over again.

So rest assured that this adventure you are on provides the perfect platform for effective, high-impact learning.

We've just reviewed how study abroad provides the platform for experiential learning, but can it also help gain knowledge about something more abstract—our own happiness?

HAPPINESS

Happiness is a very subjective term; it's in the eye of the beholder. Dan Buettner, the author of *The Blue Zones of Happiness: Lessons From the World's Happiest People*, has traveled the world to discover what makes people the happiest, and I can't help but think about study abroad when I read his findings. According to Buettner, the main components of happiness are pride, pleasure, and purpose.

> **Pride** is about how you evaluate your life overall. How satisfied are you with your job? Your family? Are you financially secure? Is your mom proud of you? Do you feel like you live your values?[2]

Buettner discusses **pleasure** and explains that "you only remember about 2 percent of your life—highs, like marriages and awards, and lows, like getting dumped. You don't remember most of the minutiae." Study abroad gives us loads of highs to remember! That's why this experience feels so intense. For someone who has just studied abroad, I wonder how much of that 2 percent comes from their time abroad. The activities in this book help you to be more mindful of what you are experiencing and aim to bring you more joy, as well as more enriching experiences.

Regarding **purpose** and its role in our happiness, Buettner asks: "How often do you use your strengths to do what you do best? How engaged are you with your life?" Study abroad helps you learn so much about yourself, which leads you to know your strengths (and weaknesses) and then use that information to help you succeed.

"SUCCESS"

Just like happiness, the word "success" has a different meaning for everyone. It could mean making "a lot" of money (but how much is a lot?),

---

2 "The Link Between Happiness, Health, and Literacy," Blue Zones, accessed December 13, 2021, https://www.bluezones.com/2018/06/happiness-lessons-from-around-the-world/.

finding a job that you love to go to every day, having a family, having time to practice your favorite hobby, or any variety of other definitions. Our cultural lens and our identity very much influence the idea of success.

➔» FAST TRACK ACT: WHAT DOES SUCCESS MEAN TO YOU?

Write down your definition of success in life. How do you think your culture and your background have shaped that? Are you happy with that definition for yourself?

No matter how you define it, I truly believe that the skills gained from study abroad can help you achieve success. I say that with confidence, because you'll have gained all of those Cultural Superpowers, which transfer to other skills in life and help you achieve whatever you want.

STATISTICS OF WHY THIS IS WORTH IT

In 2019, The Institute for International Education (IIE) released results from a wide-ranging survey of their alumni and discovered the massive impact that an international experience had on their students' futures. Here are just a few of the highlights:

- Eighty-four percent said, "I am more successful in my personal life as a result of the program."

- Eighty-one percent said, "I am more successful in my professional life as a result of the program."

- Eighty-five percent of respondents list their program experience on their résumé or CV.

- Fifty-two percent of alumni feel the program experience directly contributed to receiving a job offer at some point in their career.

- Seventy-two percent of those who have interviewed for a job have discussed some aspect of their program experience during the interview.

- Sixty-nine percent of respondents found the program positively impacted at least one aspect of their home community life.

See more at: https://p.widencdn.net/yzmz1f/IIE-Centennial -Impact-Report.

→ Putting It All Together

Back to the question I posed at the beginning of this chapter: is study abroad worth the money, time, effort, and investment you put into it?

Done right, study abroad will help you develop your resilience, adaptability, grit, and growth mindset. You will be able to see things from someone else's perspective; you will grow your emotional intelligence and learn to empathize with others. You'll learn to keep a sense of humor, in stressful situations, and tolerate ambiguity. You'll acquire skills to guide your career path and gain confidence to take on any challenge life throws at you. I'd say it's well worth it! These are lofty goals, but they are about to get loftier.

Notice that all of those amazing attributes are not just the building blocks of a happy life and a healthy psychological profile; they are also the exact core competencies and so-called soft skills that employers are looking for, or that make for great entrepreneurs, or teachers, or doctors, or pretty much any profession. Think about that future job interview and how you'll be able to confidently demonstrate the Cultural Superpowers you've gained and impress the interviewer with all of the stories you'll have to back it up.

LET'S GO DEEPER. NO, LET'S GO LOFTIER

You, yourself, stand to gain so much from this experience, but so does the world.

I truly feel that if everyone studied abroad and developed these skills, the world would be a better place. There would be fewer wars, less violence, less aggression against people different from us, and more peace and understanding. Often in this world, we are afraid of what is different, because it's unknown and unfamiliar. We shouldn't fear what we don't understand, but more, we should aim to understand why people do the things that they do before judging them. We might just realize that what we thought was the only way has different—and equally valid—interpretations.

Okay, I'll step down from my soapbox now. Before we can reach those lofty goals, we must have our feet firmly planted and do some work. Like I said, when study abroad is DONE RIGHT, all of this can happen, but it won't just happen because you go abroad. You can't rely on luck or expect it to be a passive experience. It's an active, intentional process, and paradoxically, when done right, it's difficult and frustrating; but I'm going to walk you through it and show you how it can be fun too.

DIVE DEEPER INTO...

→ Experiential Learning Theory:

David A. Kolb, *Experiential Learning: Experience as the Source of Learning and Development* (New Jersey: Pearson Education, Inc 2015).

→ Happiness:

Dan Buettner, *The Blue Zones of Happiness: Lessons From the World's Happiest People* (Washington, DC: National Geographic, 2017).

→ Persevering through challenges to gain resilience:

Angela Duckworth, *Grit: The Power of Passion and Perseverance* (New York: Scribner, 2016).

→ Skills needed for work:

"15 Soft Skills You Need To Succeed When Entering The Workforce," *Forbes*, January 22, 2019, https://www.forbes.com/sites/forbescoachescouncil /2019/01/22/15-soft-skills-you-need-to-succeed-when-entering-the-workforce/?sh=5a2fd5ef10ae.

"Unpacking Your Study Abroad Experience: Critical Reflection for Workplace Competencies," Michigan State University, March 2008, https://files.eric.ed.gov/fulltext/ED509854.pdf.

Chapter 6

YOUR NEW HOME

Making the Unfamiliar, Familiar

SCARED OF MANILA

When my wife and I arrived in Manila, the capital of the Philippines, at the start of our month-long experience of volunteering and vacationing, I can probably say that I had never been so frightened in my life. From the airport, the taxi took us to the hotel where we'd stay for just one night. As we drove, the sun had already gone down, and we were driving on small, poorly-lit streets with ramshackle huts on the side of the road and people huddled together in alleyways, doing nothing but staring at our taxi as we weaved through what felt like the middle of nowhere.

My wife and I got out of the taxi and went straight from the car door to the hotel, without looking back. Even though it wasn't that late, we didn't dare leave the hotel to get something to eat, so we stayed in, got room service, and just hung out safely indoors.

The next morning, in the daylight, we dared to walk around the block but stayed very close to each other, eyes darting back and forth, backpacks clutched to our chests—yet we still felt unsafe. We lasted about twenty minutes before heading back to the room to hang out for a couple of hours before going back to the airport for our flight down south.

Fast forward one month later—we had volunteered in the poorest village of the poorest island of the Philippines (there are 7,108 islands in the Philippines) and traveled, by ourselves, to four other cities. Now we had two days in Manila before leaving.

This time in Manila, everything felt different. As soon as we got to our hotel (not the same one), we dropped off our stuff and ventured out, seeking the side streets and off-the-beaten paths. We got lost...and as night fell, we got hungry and found some amazing little huts on the side of the street selling delicious local foods that we had tried over the past weeks. We talked to people who were huddled on the street, selling or playing games, laughing at the limited Tagalog language that we had learned, and giving recommendations for places to visit. It was fantastic.

As we walked home that night, we stopped short in our tracks...we were just outside the hotel where we had arrived one month prior. Suddenly, the unfamiliar had become familiar. The uncomfortable had become comfortable. The unusual had become usual. It was such an incredible feeling.

Adapting to a new city takes time, but this chapter's tips and activities will help speed up the process and help you gain comfort and confidence.

WE DON'T CALL IT GETTING LOST, WE CALL IT *EXPLORING*

Rebranding getting lost as exploring is another example of the positive-attitude mindset from Chapter 3.

I know it's not always easy. Look at me in Manila! That trip was after studying and interning abroad, living abroad, and working abroad for years, but I was still shocked, scared, and withdrawn that first day.

The first few days, weeks, or more can have you asking yourself why you even did this. Why did you leave everything that was comfortable and familiar, to feel like this? I certainly felt that way. It's normal. And it's actually a good thing. Feeling like that makes you that much more confident when you overcome it and thrive on the other side.

The problem is that, if you are in a state of culture shock, the learning stops and it's hard to allow info in.

Feeling comfortable in your immediate surroundings—starting by getting to know your city—is the tip of the iceberg, and it's incredibly important.

How do you make the unfamiliar, familiar? The unknown, known? What can you do?

→》 FAST TRACK ACT: THE CULTURAL BLUEPRINT

This is an activity that you can do on your own or in a group with people from back home (the same city or region as you).

Example: If I were a student from Chicago going to do an internship abroad in Milan, Italy, for a summer (which I was!), for this activity, I would imagine a student from Italy—let's call her Sofia—going to Chicago for a summer. My task would be to create a list of activities that Sofia should do to really get to know the culture—*the culture of Chicago and American culture*—and to learn what the people are like.

Now, for you, substitute Chicago for the city you come from and substitute Milan, Italy, for the city and country you are going to. For example, if you are going to study in Prague, Czech Republic, for four months and you are from Minneapolis, Minnesota, you should work with that info.

Step 1: You will write down all of the things you would tell Sofia to do, see, experience, and eat.

Step 2: You will write down what she will learn about the values and beliefs of that culture.

STEP 1:

Write down all of the things that you would tell Sofia to…

- Do
- See
- Experience
- Eat

…in your city, region, and country, so she really gets to know the culture of where you are from.

You might need a good twenty to thirty minutes to complete Step 1.

Using the iceberg metaphor, these are the observable things above the water. Write down some of your own, first, then see my examples below.

STEP 2:

Only after finishing Step 1, for each of those things you wrote down, write down what she will learn about the values and beliefs of that culture. Using the iceberg metaphor, these are the implicit aspects below the water.

This may take you longer than the first step.

Essentially, your goal is to help Sofia iceberg everything she will do, see, experience, and eat, and then she can learn what the values and beliefs of your culture are.

Don't worry if you can't come up with something in Step 2 for each of your suggestions! It would be surprising if you could. Remember, building up your iceberging muscle takes time, so if you only get 10–20 percent right now, that's totally fine and expected.

Here's an example of what I would have said for Chicago and American culture.

My Example with Step 1 and Step 2 Combined

What would I recommend that Sofia do, see, eat, experience, etc.? What can Sofia learn about US culture by doing these things? What can she learn that Americans value, enjoy, and feel is "normal"?

Note: the iceberging done here is purposely not going as deep as we will go in later chapters, since we are still just getting started and learning to build our iceberging muscles.

I recommend Sofia…

- **Meet people her own age.** When she meets people her own age, she has a cultural treasure trove waiting to be discovered. It's the opportunity to learn about so many aspects of culture that don't come from a book or a museum but from a real live person. Of all of those things on this list, meeting people her own age is one of the best things she can do. How should she do this?

This is so important to your time abroad that I want to stop for a second before we go further. Making local friends abroad is one of the quickest and best ways to have the most incredible experience possible. But how do you do it?

First, take the initiative. Forget any thought that locals will flock to you, to become your best friend, just because you are a foreigner. You are the one who needs to take the initiative.

Here are some tips:

- If you are at a local university, talk to your classmates and start by asking to study together.

- Offer to start a language exchange with someone: you help them with their English if they help you learn the language of that country.

- Use apps that connect you with people who are in your vicinity. Some of my students use dating apps to meet people their age.

- Join a sports club.

- Remember Meetup.com, where people interested in some activity find others who are also interested, and they meet up.

- **Attend a local sports game!** Go see a Chicago Cubs game (sorry White Sox fans) and observe what baseball is like, or a basketball game, or a hockey game. Even if she doesn't understand the sport, she will see that going to a sporting event in the US is as much about what is happening outside the game as the game itself. We can be entertained, the entire time, by the jumbotron, the dancers, the mascot, the beer, the food, the souvenirs, etc. Compare that to a football (soccer) game in Italy, where they don't serve alcohol, there are no cheerleaders or dancers, there is no jumbotron playing advertisements and showing cartoons race each other around. She will see that fans of the opposing teams sit right next to each other and act friendly, in contrast to soccer stadiums around the world, where fans of opposing teams might sit in a separate section, which is often completely sealed off and protected by plexiglass and police. So she learns that Americans value being entertained, the social aspect, and being friendly with strangers and that Americans are very good at marketing and selling.

- **Experience tailgating** before a college American Football game. This goes along with the other sports experience above, in that the entertainment and the social aspect of the game start even BEFORE the game—hours before. She'll see that Americans like to wear all kinds of clothes and buy paraphernalia to support their team and feel like they are part of that team. Even alumni who graduated forty years before still support their college and feel like they belong to that school. By comparison, at many European universities, the students say they "wouldn't be caught dead in a school sweatshirt, because those are only for tourists." Again, at US tailgating events, you'll get fans of opposing teams hanging out together, drinking, and exchanging friendly banter.

- **Go to the Illinois State Fair.** You wanna get some culture shock? Definitely do this! (Even *I* get culture shock when I go to a state fair). Check out the food that people eat. See how people dress. See all the different types of things that people can buy there. She will see that Americans are very creative with their foods (i.e., deep-fried peanut butter and jelly or corn dogs on a stick. Corn dog on a stick did not seem abnormal to me until I took my wife to the fair and she had never seen anything like it before.) She can appreciate the creativity and ability to sell all kinds of food—the more gluttonous, the better at the state fair. She'll see that people dress very informally and comfortably.

- **Get a drink at a Starbucks or a local café.** She will see that many people there are sitting at individual tables, with their computers, working. They can get up to go to the bathroom and leave everything there at the table unattended (depending on the location). This would be unheard of (or very foolish) in many big cities around the world because their belongings could easily get stolen. She'll also see how some people just walk in the door, and their order is ready for them because they ordered previously, through an app. This will show the convenience that Americans value. Much more about coffee, food, and drink in Chapters 11 and 12.

- **Go to a backyard BBQ.** She will see that Americans value friendliness and openness to strangers. Many of my European friends have commented that they can't believe how friendly Americans are and how quick someone is to invite you to their house when they've just met you. She would also observe what small talk is like for Americans—what are some of the first questions that get asked and how quickly people give you personal details.

AN AMERICAN ENCOUNTER IN BARCELONA

I was walking on a street in the center of Barcelona, when I came across an older American couple, looking lost, with a paper map open. I stopped to offer them some help, and I kid you not, in the four minutes that we talked, I found out that:

1. They were from Wisconsin.

2. They just recently retired.

3. They sold their house, which meant they had some money to travel, so they came to Spain.

4. They have two kids.

5. One of the kids studied abroad in Argentina (this came up because the first question they asked me was what I do, and I said I work in Study Abroad).

6. That the son who studied in Argentina now lives in Colorado, because he was married to an Argentinean woman but it didn't work out so they got divorced.

7. Their daughter still lives in Wisconsin and is in her thirties and works at a bank but is still trying to find her way.

8. And they found out (because they asked) whether I was married, had kids, and what my wife does for a living.

9. All of this in four minutes. I swear I thought they were going to invite my family and me to visit them in Wisconsin! This type of friendliness, sharing of personal information, and asking for personal information might seem "totally normal" to some people yet "totally intrusive" to others from another culture.

~~~~~~

- **Get a meal at a drive-through of a fast-food restaurant.** She will see that many people working there are younger, even in high school or college, and working at night—compared to many Europeans who don't get a job until they are older. She'll also see the convenience that Americans value, with a drive-through that allows them to eat on the go while doing other things.

- **Eat a meal at the house of a local family.** She'll see how a family interacts and communicates, what a US house looks like and how it's decorated, and what they do in their leisure time. She'll experience what kind of food they cook at home and how children talk with parents and vice-versa.

- **Go grocery food shopping at a Costco.** She'll see a world of difference, with shopping, versus in Italy. The huge packages, the food sold in bulk, and the gigantic carts allow people to buy food for the next several weeks, rather than just a couple of days, as is typical in Italy.

- **Take a weekend trip down to the state capital, Springfield, Illinois,** to learn about Illinois-and-US history. She will get information about the life of Abraham Lincoln, which may spark curiosity to learn about the terrible legacy of slavery in the US, and see where the first Black president, Barack Obama, started his political career. The history will help her understand why the culture is like it is now, based on past struggles certain groups have had, different leaders of the country, and what their time in office still means today.

- **Experience a traditional seasonal festival**, like a Fourth of July party, Thanksgiving, or Halloween. A traditional festival gives her a lens into what the culture celebrates and why. What is important to them? Who are their heroes, and what are the important events in history? Is it a religious culture?

- **Attend a US university class on a campus.** If Sofia can attend a university class on campus, she'll observe how students dress. Students dress down on US campuses much more than in Europe. Wearing flip flops, pajama bottoms, sweatpants, and hats backward is not typical in Italy. She'll also observe how students and teachers interact, the authority a university professor has (or doesn't), and how the students treat the professor.

STEP 3:

YOUR Cultural Blueprint.

The Cultural Blueprint activity is brilliant because it motivates you to reflect on your own culture and what that means about your values and beliefs, but it also has a hidden benefit:

You now have a blueprint for what YOU can do abroad to learn about the host culture. All of the things you told Sofia to do, you should be doing in your new city and country.

- Meet people your own age!

- Attend a local sports game. Whether that's football, cricket, curling, or jai-alai, go see a sport that you know or that you've never heard of before.

- Go tailgating (or the equivalent of tailgating). Does something like this exist where you are studying? If so, join in.

- Go to a State Fair or the equivalent.

- Get a drink at a local café and see how they drink coffee, tea, or something similar.

- Go to a backyard BBQ.

- Get a meal at a drive-through restaurant...or don't! In Barcelona, a city of 1.6 million residents, there is exactly one drive-through restaurant—a McDonald's as you drive out of the city. So the idea here is to eat like the locals do. If they don't eat at drive-throughs, then go eat the way they do. Go and observe all of the things that stick out to you.

- Get a meal at the house of a local family.

- Go grocery food shopping the way that the locals do.

- Take a weekend trip to a place that has historical or political significance. Find out why it's significant to them and what it still means for them today.

- Experience a traditional, seasonal festival—there is so much fun to be had and so much culture to be absorbed there.

- Attend a university class, especially if it uses the city as the classroom and teaches you about the city through history, culture, music, art, architecture, etc.

→ ACT: Add to Your Cultural Blueprint as You Go Along

While you're abroad, you'll undoubtedly come up with more cool activities to add to a cultural blueprint. I'd encourage you to add them to your list as you go. I can almost guarantee that you will become a mentor, for a future student going abroad, and your blueprint will help them.

→ ACT: Go Back to Your Cultural Blueprint before You Go Home

At the end of your study abroad experience, go back to this exercise and review your answers to Step 2. Are you now able to better understand what values and beliefs could be gained about your culture, from doing those activities? How much have your iceberging muscles grown?

→ ACT: NESW, North East South West

I've seen too many students get comfortable with one path to their school or internship and stick with it every time they go. We tend to be creatures of habit, and once we learn a route, we feel most comfortable sticking to it. My challenge to them and to you is to start taking a new route once you get comfortable.

Sometimes just taking one street over from the one that you are used to helps you find a hidden gem in the city, a store that has the perfect thing for you, a café or restaurant that becomes your new favorite, or other places you would not have otherwise found.

To systematically make sure you are doing this, you could use Google Maps or a similar app to track where you've been, so you can see, at a glance, where you *haven't* been. Then go to those places you haven't been to. Or you could go old-school and get a paper map and a highlighter and, at the end of every day, highlight the streets you've explored. I had one student do this, and at the end of her semester, she had a highlighted map, which she framed and put up on her wall back home as a beautiful memory of places explored.

→ ACT: Do a Silent Tour

When you find a new neighborhood or area you want to explore, try doing it by yourself without listening to music or anything. Just walk around, in silence, to heighten your observation. You'll be amazed at what you see when you are looking for the details. Pay attention to languages, spoken and written; how people dress; how people interact; the age of people; who is hanging out together and who isn't; what is getting sold in the stores; how old the neighborhood is; and what statues and plaques are there, as well as who are they dedicated to. You can also pay attention to gender relations, personal space, family dynamics, architecture, marketing and advertising, and the use of public space.

Once you have done this in one neighborhood, go check out the others. Many cities tend to have different sections, each with their own unique character.

→ ACT: Join Guided Tours

Doing silent tours by yourself has its merit but so do guided tours. When you can learn the history of a building, or the events that took place there, or the symbolism of a piece of artwork, usually your appreciation for, and understanding of, that location increases tenfold.

For example, there is this out-of-the-way plaza in Barcelona behind a major tourist area that has a church with pockmarks on the wall. The pockmarks look like wear and tear, and you would probably walk right past it. But then you find out that they were created by bombs the Italians, by Mussolini's orders, dropped and directed towards the people of Barcelona, during the Spanish Civil War in the 1930s, which makes it more meaningful. What are those hidden gems you can find in your city?

→ ACT: Get a Guidebook and Use Podcasts

When you can't join a guided tour, you can make one yourself by buying a guidebook (or checking one out from a local library) or listening to a podcast with guided tours by geolocation.

→ ACT: Write Your Own Guidebook for Future Students

Imagine your best friend is going to study abroad in your city; what would you recommend that they see and do, based on what you've learned on your own, on tours, or in classes? Write them a mini guidebook with suggested places.

DIVE DEEPER INTO...
→ City and country guides:

Lonely Planet travel resources and guides, https://www.lonelyplanet.com.

Rick Steve's City travel resources and guides, https://www.ricksteves.com.

Chapter 7

ICEBERGING NATIONAL CULTURE

GOOD INTENTIONS. WRONG RESULT.

I screwed up on my second day on the job in Barcelona. Here I am, thinking I'm a big shot, ready for this new intercultural life working abroad—I'd studied abroad twice, in two different countries, and interned in a third country; but I still had a lot to learn.

I just wanted to show my passion for what we were doing in study abroad: combining two great countries, the US and Spain; bringing students over from the US; and helping them fall in love with Spain as I had. To demonstrate that passion, I brought in a mini US flag and a mini Spanish flag and proudly displayed them, together, on my desk, in a nice stand.

My boss, a Catalan man, walked in, saw the flags, stopped short, and said, "*What is that?!*" I explained my excitement for international education and my love of these two countries. He mumbled something in disbelief and then proclaimed that he planned to bring in his Catalan-independence flag and that I should rethink what I had on display.

Here's what I didn't learn in all my time studying in Madrid and traveling Spain: that Catalonia, the region of Spain with Barcelona as its capital, has been fighting for its independence from Spain for hundreds of years, and to many people in Catalonia (although not all), the Spanish flag is a symbol of entrenched and relentless oppression against the Catalan people, language, and culture. Oops. Not a good start.

On top of all that, George W. Bush was president in the US and was one of the least popular US presidents, from a Spanish perspective, for several reasons, including the war in Afghanistan and impending war in Iraq, so the US flag did me no favors either.

~~~~~~

This cultural incident taught me that I should have learned more about the history and politics of the region I was in, but it also showed me something about US national culture: how much we take pride in our flag. Many schools still have kids say the Pledge of Allegiance to the flag, every morning, which very few other countries do. Pay attention next time you watch any movie made in the US; you will almost ALWAYS see a US flag in it; drive down your average suburban street, and you'll see the flag hanging on houses, fast-food restaurants, and other stores. The American flag is flown and often saluted, at virtually every sporting event. This happens in some other countries around the world, but not usually to the extent that it has come to be expected in the US.

In 2016, the organization YouGov polled adults in nineteen countries about this question: "Do you think your country is the best in the world?" Guess who came in number one—USA with 41 percent of people saying it is the best country in the world and 32 percent who believe it is "better than most countries." Compare that to France, where only 5 percent of French people said that "(their) country was the best in the world."[3]

National culture is what we grew up believing to be true, and it's what gives us a collective sense of pride. Pride in your country is fine, but be mindful of how other countries might respond if you brag that what you do in your country is better than how it's done in the country you are studying in.

This is important because that will tint your cultural lens, based on how you feel about your own country, and potentially how other countries

---

3   "YouGov Survey Results—Topline Findings," YouGov, 2016, https://d25d2506sfb94s.cloudfront.net/cumulus_uploads/document/71wl1vs4ii/International%20toplines_W.pdf.

will see you. I've had several discussions and debates with non-Americans who say: "You think that the US is the best country in the world, but what about X, Y, and Z," where they point out what they see as problems—some of which I agree with; with others, I keep in mind that two people can look at the same thing and interpret it differently.

Study abroad helps you learn about the history, politics, geography, social etiquette, and more of a national culture, so you can avoid offending people and discover so much about yourself in the process. It will help you understand why people do what they do, which, in turn, helps you to adapt to the new rules.

→ ACT: Big Moments in Your Nation's History

Step 1: If an international student was going to study in your home country, what historical events or moments would you want them to know to help them understand the culture and not make a mistake like I did above?

For example, if we were talking about the US, I would say they would need to know about the Civil Rights Movement, the history of slavery, the Revolutionary War, the Civil War, 9/11, and the different waves of immigration to the US, to name a few.

Step 2: Do the same for the country you are going to. There are two ways of doing it. One is to simply do research. Find books or websites to give you background. The other is our next ACT and, in my opinion, is a lot more fun and gives you much more insight.

THE ONE-HOUR AMBASSADOR

My wife and I went to Tallinn, Estonia for vacation one summer, and we fell in love with it because of a *one-hour conversation* with a young Estonian woman.

During a walking tour of the city, we spent most of the time in the back, talking to Hanna, who was twenty-one years old, from Tallinn, and training to be a tour guide. That one hour of getting to know her, and her willingness to answer all our questions (you can imagine I had a lot!) endeared her, as well as her country and culture, to us.

I enjoyed that conversation so much that I created an activity around it.

➔≫ FAST TRACK ACT: THE ONE-HOUR AMBASSADOR

Find someone university-age from the local culture, ask for an hour of their time, and ask these questions:

- At what age do people tend to move out of their parents' homes?

- What are you studying and why?

- What job do you plan to have?

- What would you rather have: more vacation time or more money?

- Do you follow politics?

- What do you do in your free time?

- What is the nightlife like here?

- What was your first job, if you've worked already?

- How do you get around?

- What's a typical vacation like for someone from here?

- Tell me about your experience in high school (or the equivalent).

- What does your typical day's schedule look like during the week? On the weekend?

- Do people your age date? What's the dating culture like?

- What is the alcohol culture like here?

- Is this a religious country?

- What's a typical meal? Do you have any restaurant recommendations to get to know typical food?

- What does (your) country think about (my country)? You might want to add, "Be honest; I can take it," then try not to get defensive.

- Do you think people here are more likely to follow the theory of "live to work" or "work to live"?

Here's what I absolutely loved about this activity. After that one hour, we learned so much about her culture, and as a bonus, we learned tons of practical tips on what to do, eat, and see there. It was like our own mini Cultural Blueprint.

Since she also asked us questions, we turned into ambassadors for our countries.

Just in that one hour, the world became a little smaller, and we got to see things from her perspective and share our perspective, all of which made us reflect more on our own cultures. Maybe it should be called the "one-hour iceberg."

MORE ASPECTS OF NATIONAL CULTURE

Related to history, what can a country's politics and geography tell you about its culture?

An international student coming to the US, for example, would have to understand the deep fractures in our two-party (Republican–Democrat) system to comprehend how people act today. I think this is especially important for American students going abroad, because US politics is front-page material of most newspapers around the world, so students often say that the locals know more about US politics than they do. You may want to brush up on US politics, so you don't feel in the dark.

→ Geography, the Weather, and Its Influence on Culture

The weather is also a major factor in how people behave. There is certainly a "Mediterranean culture" (resulting from the hot weather) encouraging people to spend more time outdoors. This affects everything from the size of houses to spending habits at bars and restaurants, and even views on life.

In colder climates with less sunlight, we know that S.A.D., Seasonal Affective Disorder, is a real problem leading to greater levels of depression. These countries have come up with methods of combating the "winter blues," such as natural-light lamps, giant mirrors, light clinics, and positive psychology.

I know several people who have gone to live in the UK and loved the experience, but the first thing they complain about is rarely seeing a blue sky (especially if that's what they are used to), and it truly affects their adaptation.

This is a favorite example of mine: when I went to Denmark, I was fascinated to learn about the concept of "hygge." Hygge is a word that's difficult to translate, but it has to do with the coziness and comfort of where you are, compared to somewhere less cozy. It could be that there is a cold, rainy storm outside, but you are inside with candles lit, under a warm, comfortable blanket, with a fire going. Denmark uses more candles per capita than any other country in the world![4]

Understanding how the weather influences culture can help you fit in or make you stand out. I was in Seattle once, and it started lightly drizzling, so I busted out my giant umbrella, and I was the only one! Everyone else was so used to a light drizzle that they didn't even bother or had jackets with hoods on them. I certainly did not fit in then.

National culture also consists of knowing the heroes. Who are the people—current or historical—that are looked up to, and why?

→ ACT: We Could Be Heroes

Step 1: Write down who the heroes of your home culture are and why you think that's the case. What does it tell you about the culture's values?

Step 2: Find out who the heroes are of the culture you are studying in. Again, you could do this by research or, better yet, by asking some locals.

When I last visited the US, I went to a baseball game where we were all asked to stand and recognize a hero—a woman in the army who had just returned from a tour abroad. She got a standing ovation. This has never happened at any sporting event I've been to around the world.

In the US, we might also think of heroes like Dr. Martin Luther King, Jr., Michael Jordan, Steve Jobs, or the Donut King. Who is the Donut King, you ask? I only know because I watched a documentary on Ted Ngoy, the man who is singularly responsible for 90 percent of the donut shops in California. He was a Cambodian refugee who came to the US with nothing and became a rags-to-riches story, resulting in then-president George H.W. Bush presenting him with a Presidential Award for "achieving the American dream."

Why is the American Dream such a value in the US?

---

4   "Cocoa by Candlelight: Why Do So Many Foreigners Want to Copy Denmark?" *The Economist*, September 29, 2016, https://www.economist.com/europe/2016/09/29/cocoa-by-candlelight.

→ Individualism

We cannot talk about US culture without talking about Individualism. The US is the most individualistic country in the world—we know this based on much research, especially that of the late famous cultural guru Geerte Hofstede.[5] This means that we value "picking ourselves up by our bootstraps," working hard on our own to be successful (and successful usually means making money and demonstrating that with having lots of stuff), competition, and winning. It means that we are encouraged to self-promote and self-enhance, and we are more willing to take risks to prove our worth. Our parents often tell us how special we are—encouraging a sense that we are unique.

It also means that we are encouraged to leave the house at eighteen years old, to go to university in a different city or state, move again for a job, and move again with our families.

This individualism seeps into so many aspects of our behavior, from promoting ourselves well (some call it bragging), to vanity license plates, to the way we order food.

When we iceberg many behaviors in the US and ask, "Why do they DO that?!" diving down to the bottom, we often land at this high ranking on the individualism scale.

→ Collectivism

The opposite end of the spectrum is Collectivism, defined by cultures that don't want to stick out individually; they worry about the team or collective first, before the individual, and it's more important to maintain harmony than to compete individually.

Let's look at education. For example, if you are going to class abroad in a more collectivistic culture, rather than individualistic, the students in that culture may be more likely to help each other out, even if that means

---

5   "Country Comparison," Hofstede Insights, accessed July 14, 2021, https://www.hofstede-insights.com/country-comparison/the-usa/.

copying on a test. In the US we are taught to be honorable (notice the value placement, "honorable" by US cultural standards) and not cheat on a test or copy off someone else. In fact, if you have studied hard, all semester, for a class and your friend has been lazy and decided to skip class, and then asks to copy your test to get a good grade, most likely you would say hell no because *you've* put in the hard work. Spanish friends have told me that they would happily "copy"—or work in a team with other students—to get the right answer on a test.

We can't just call these students dishonorable using our cultural lens. This also has a cultural explanation, which a Spanish professor once told me: "In the US, you test to see what a student knows; in Spain, we test to find out what a student *doesn't* know. So we put difficult and obscure questions to see if we can catch the student out." Having taken the Spanish driver's license exam, I can attest to that. There were questions, from the small sidenote on page 132 of the 250-page textbook, about how a carburetor works! In addition, in collectivist societies, you help your in-groups instead of just helping yourself. This might be why students in Spain decide that it's okay to help each other out on tests, something that is difficult to understand from a US cultural lens.

→ ACT: Individualism vs. Collectivism

Google Geerte Hofstede's cultural dimension of Individualism vs. Collectivism. Where does the country where you are studying sit on the scale? How might this explain some of your observations and interactions?

This brings us to another important aspect of national culture—philosophy of life: work to live or live to work?

WORK TO LIVE OR LIVE TO WORK?

When they offered me my dream job to work in Barcelona, it came at a price. Literally. I was facing a significant pay cut if I took the job. Salaries in Spain are much lower in general than in the US. As I mulled over the decision, I thought about it this way: if I stayed at my job in Chicago, I would use my two weeks of vacation (yes, *only* two weeks per year compared to starting with four weeks) to go to Spain. So it made a lot more sense to take a pay cut and live all year round in the place that, otherwise, I would have spent money to fly to, pay for a hotel, and barely get a taste of the good life before having to get right back on a plane and go home.

Looking at it that way made it clear that the only decision was to take the job, despite some of my friends asking: "Why would you go work in Spain when you can make more money staying in the US?"

Little did I know then that I had based my decision on one important aspect of national culture: do you live to work or work to live?

When I worked in Chicago and met friends out in the city, socially, one of the first questions they'd ask me was: "How's work going?" I would be happy to tell them that work was really busy; I had to get into work early that morning and just came straight out for drinks, from work, because I had to stay late since so much was going on. Their response? Oh, that's great! Sounds like things are going well then.

That question—*how's work?*—and answer—*busy*—were expected, reinforced, and rewarded.

So when I moved to Barcelona and would meet some new friends out for drinks, I was in for a shock when nothing went as I expected and my ingrained responses were not rewarded or reinforced.

We were out at a bar, and a friend would introduce me to one of her Spanish friends. During our get-to-know-you chitchat, I would be waiting and waiting for them to ask me what I do. After asking where I was from, how I was enjoying Barcelona, what plans I had for my time in Spain, whether I was a Barça fan, etc., I was getting itchy for them to ask me where I worked. But they didn't.

The American in me was dying to talk about work, so I brought it up any way possible. "Yeah, I really like Barcelona. I wish I had more time to visit it, though, but I haven't really yet because there is so much going on at work. I work with a study abroad company, and even though we just opened up, we have tons of students, many more than any of us expected (*and here comes the part I was looking forward to saying to get that reinforcement*), so things are really busy. I usually have to go in early, and I just barely made it here, because I had to stay late to get stuff done today."

Their response? "Oh, that's too bad. What a shame you have to spend so much time at work."

What?! The exact opposite reaction from what I was expecting.

Whenever I tried to bring the conversation back to work, I could see their eyes glaze over. So what did I do? I stopped talking about work so much in that context. It wasn't expected, reinforced, or rewarded.

Don't get me wrong; Spaniards do work hard, and I know many people here who are entrepreneurial, talk about work, and feel proud of what they do and what they have created, but even they seem to be able to separate their work from their personal life more than Americans.

Why?

Let's iceberg it, shall we?

Why do Americans talk about work so much? If you've ever taken a psychology class, you've seen Maslow's hierarchy of needs. At the very top of the pyramid is Self-Actualization. This is the idea that there is something in our lives that defines us and makes us feel whole. It could be religion, family, our tribe, or any number of things. Studies have shown that, in the US, what we most aspire to and what makes us feel self-actualized is **work**. Our jobs. Our jobs have the opportunity to define us and make us feel great.

LET'S TALK SHOP

In America, one of the very first questions that adults ask each other, when they meet for the first time is, *What do you do?* And one of the very first questions, after you've known each other for a while, is, *How is work?* But this is not the case everywhere around the world.

A friend of mine from southern Spain went to a party, with his American wife, back in the US. At one point, they got split up at the party, and he went to his wife later, sounding very confused, and said:

"Everyone keeps asking me what I do, but when I tell them, 'I like to play the electric bass, hike, and travel to as many countries as possible,' they look very confused. Then they start telling me where they work. What's going on?"

His wife responded: "No, they are asking you what your JOB is, not what you like to do as a hobby."

He said, "Why would they want to know where I work? It's much less interesting than what I do outside of work."

And it's not as if he has a boring job: he works for a multinational company that makes machines that can do complicated operations, and he has a degree in biology, but if you iceberg his behavior, you see that he believes that it's much more interesting to talk about his hobbies than his work.

Another of my Spanish friends says she feels insulted when, upon first meeting people, they ask her what she does—like they are judging her right away and will make inferences about her, immediately, by her profession—she says that she would never ask anyone what they do for a living.

All of this boils down to a fundamental cultural question: **Do we work to live or do we live to work?**

Does a culture see work as our form of self-actualization? Do they talk about work all the time? Do they want to hear about other people's work? Do they put in a lot of extra hours and think about work all the time?

Or are the people happy to have a job that allows them to live the life they want to lead?

Americans even have a hard time taking vacations. In 2018, Americans left—unused—a combined total of 768 million days of paid time off, and we've been called "the no-vacation nation."[6] Americans invented the term "micro-cation," meaning taking short-and-sweet breaks, so as not to feel so guilty being away from work.

Even when we are on vacation, we still check emails and messages.

Why do we still work on vacation? We value hard work, as we've said, but we also value being available and helpful if a colleague needs us to get their work done. We value productivity. That show of dedication to work might eventually help us move up the corporate ladder, which brings us back to the American Dream.

~~~~~~

GREEK FISHERMAN

You may have heard the fable of the Greek fisherman and the Ivy League–educated MBA CEO before: (Note: there is no known author of the original tale, so I've taken a few creative liberties to update it).

A powerful CEO of a large American business takes a short holiday to a small Greek island. While the CEO is taking an early morning walk along the beach, she comes across a fisherman lounging in his boat docked with several freshly caught fish hanging down. The CEO says, "How long did it take you to catch those fish?"

"Not that long," replied the Greek fisherman.

"Then why didn't you stay out longer and catch more?" asked the CEO.

"I've caught enough for what I need for my family today and tomorrow. Now I'll spend the rest of my day with my kids, have a long lunch with my wife, and take a little nap before hanging out with my friends this afternoon," said the fisherman.

The CEO laughs and says, "Sir, I am a successful businesswoman with an MBA from Harvard, and I can give you some advice that would make you incredibly successful. If you stayed out there longer, you could catch five times the amount of fish and sell them for a small profit."

---

6   Hannah Sampson, "What Does America Have Against Vacation?" *The Washington Post*, August 28, 2019, https://www.washingtonpost.com/travel/2019/08/28/what-does-america-have-against-vacation/.

"Ok, then what?" asked the fisherman.

"You do that long enough to make the money you need to buy another boat and hire some help. You and your team start catching enough fish to sell directly to the market."

"Ok, then what do I do?"

"Then when you have enough money, you build your own fish market and open a restaurant, with you as the personal brand behind this powerful story you're building. You start diversifying and making money in these different areas: restaurant, wholesale, direct to market—who knows what other offshoots you could come up with."

"Ok, then what?"

"I've seen it before; the restaurant becomes so popular that you move to the big city to open up a chain of them, and you're making money through other peoples' work. Eventually, you have the fish empire of Greece, and you have made millions!"

"Ok, great. How long do you think that would take?"

"I think you could do it in twenty to twenty-five years tops."

"Ok, then what?"

"Then," says the CEO with a smile, "you can retire, live near the beach, spend time with your grandchildren, have long lunches with your wife, take naps when you want, and hang out with your friends."

~~~~~~

The last time you asked someone how they were doing, how did they respond? When I return to the US and ask, I bet they will tell me that they are "busy" within the first sentence. Busy. We are all busy all the time. How are you doing? Good, good, busy but good.

Why do we say this so much? Look no further than our first definition of culture: "What is expected, reinforced, and rewarded within a particular social group."

In Spain, however, a common response to *"Qué tal?"* (how are you doing?) is *"Bien, trabajando un poquito"* (Good, just working a little bit). So, yes, there is work, but it's just a little bit (even if they are actually working a lot, it's not something to brag about).

WHY? IN THE US, WE VALUE PRODUCTIVITY

For one thing, we know that other Americans value hard work, so it's our way of connecting with that other person and building the relationship. When we iceberg it even deeper, we find that Americans highly **value productivity**. We love to be productive. Being busy is a way that we feel productive.

When I ask a room full of students how many of them use a checklist of some sort for the things they need to get done, almost everybody raises their hands. When I ask them how many still use one, even on the weekends, about 60 percent of them still raise their hands. The weekEND. The end of the week. The end of the workweek. They say it makes them feel productive and they have so much to do that they need to keep track of it all.

Why do Americans have this desire to be productive? Does it come from our history of being founded on a Protestant work ethic? Does it come from our insatiable desire for social mobility and knowing that where there is a will, there's a way?

Or is it that work is the way to make money, which allows us to have more stuff?

→ ACT: Do You Live to Work or Work to Live?

Step 1: Think about yourself, your parents, friends, partners, family members, coworkers, etc. Do they work to live or live to work? How do you know?

Step 2: What about the culture you are studying in? Do they live to work or work to live? How do you know? If it's different from the culture you come from, how does that make you feel?

SOCIAL ETIQUETTE

What seems rude to us might seem perfectly polite to someone else. As with most of these examples, we can even see differences between regions of the same country, which is certainly true within the US. When I was visiting New Orleans, I got in a taxi with a colleague of mine who is from the southern US, and since I'm from Chicago, which is definitely not the South, I experienced some culture shock. The taxi driver asked me my name; I said, "Rich," and she said, "Welcome to New Orleans, Mr. Rich." I told her, "Just Rich is fine, no need for the 'Mr.'" She was a little taken aback and said, "I can't call you that; that would be rude." Mind you, she was older than I was! I said, "Don't worry, I don't think it's rude," and she explained that she understood, but she couldn't bring herself not to say "Mr."—that's how she would address any adult.

As we headed to lunch with some staff from an HBCU (Historically Black College and University), my colleague mentioned that I should definitely refer to them as Ms. Kara or Mr. Steve, except for the director, who had a PhD, and that I must call her Dr. Price, not Ms. Price. She told me that in the African American community, when someone has earned a doctorate, they are always referred to as Dr.

Let's Iceberg that, shall we?

Historically, African Americans in the US have been dramatically and systematically left out of the same educational opportunities as White people. The unequal access to opportunities and quality education starts at a very young age, but then it becomes even more difficult to get into colleges and then graduate programs, making it an especially noteworthy achievement to earn a PhD. Therefore, the Dr. label is essential.

→ ACT: Photojournalism Assignment

It's time for my favorite question again, but this time with a twist.

What's something that has stuck out to you and made you say, "This would never happen in my home country?"

This time, instead of writing it down, I want you to take a photo of it (where culturally appropriate), then write down why you think it does happen in the host culture and why it doesn't happen where you come from.

Photo by Kevin Strandberg

My example would be this *correfoc* (fire run), which takes place in Catalonia. People dress up as devils and run down the street shooting industrial-strength giant sparklers/fireworks. Locals run in and out of the "fire parade." Parents encourage their young kids to do it too. I can't see it ever taking place in the US, because of the aversion to health-and-safety risks that lead to lawsuits.

In Catalonia, I think it's allowed because it is a festival with historical significance, there have been relatively few injuries, and because Spain is not such a litigious society, so there is not a threat of lawsuits stopping people from doing these things that seem dangerous from an American cultural lens.

HOW ALL OF THIS WILL HELP YOU: KNOWLEDGE, SKILLS, AND AWARENESS

By understanding national cultures—the one you're going to and your own—you become **aware** of these differences, acquire the **knowledge** to identify what is normal to you in comparison or contrast to the other cultures, and gain the **skills** necessary to bridge that gap. This helps you develop superpowers of adaptability to so many different situations—like a cultural chameleon. And those skills don't just come in handy when you live in another country; they will help you navigate the different cultures within your own country.

DIVE DEEPER INTO...

→ Research on cultural differences across countries:

Geert Hofstede, Gert Jan Hofstede, and Michael Minkov, *Cultures and Organizations: Software of the Mind* (New York City: McGraw Hill Professional, 2010).

→ Individualism:

Steven Dubner, "The US is Just Different—So Let's Stop Pretending We're Not," *Freakonomics: The Hidden Side of Everything,* July 14, 2021, Episode 469, https://freakonomics.com/podcast/season-10-episode-49/.

Steven Dubner, "The Pros and Cons of America's (Extreme) Individualism," *Freakonomics: The Hidden Side of Everything,* July 21, 2021, Episode 470, https://freakonomics.com/podcast/the-pros-and-cons-of-americas-extreme-individualism-ep-470-2/.

Chapter 8

LEARN TO SPEAK THE LANGUAGE

was in a class full of students from over fifteen countries, who were about to embark on separate study abroad journeys to different places. I started my talk like this:

Me: Hi, where are you from?

Student 1: China

Me: *Ni hao!* (Hello)

Student 1: *Look of pleasant surprise*

Me: Where are you from?

Student 2: Morocco

Me: *"Salaam Alekhem"* (Good day)

Student 2: *big smile*

Me: You?

Student 3: Israel

Me: *Shalom* (Hello, goodbye, or peace)

Student 3: *nod of approval*

Me: You?

Student 4: I'm from California

Me: Oh, hey, what's up?

Student 4: *laughter*

Me: You?

Student 5: Poland

Me: *Jenkioie* (Thank you)

Student 5: *slightly confused why I'd say "thank you," but appreciative*

Me: You?

Student 6: Korea

Me: *Ne salang he* (I love you)

Student: *confusion and blushing*

Me: You?

Student 7: Nigeria

Me: *Mo gbo Yoruba* (A close but mistaken attempt to say, "I understand Yoruba," which is one of the languages of Nigeria)

Student: *smiles and says something I didn't understand in Yoruba*

Me: Uhm, sorry, that's actually the only thing I can say in Yoruba, which often gets me in trouble because they keep talking to me, and I have no idea what they are saying.

Laughter from everyone.

I have studied many languages, but the point of my introduction at that talk was not to show off; it was that **when you can speak even just a few words of someone's language, you can connect and endear yourself to them**.

Our language(s) is/are a large part of our identity. When you learn to speak someone else's language, you validate their identity and show that you want to learn more about them and their culture.

Even though some of my responses above made no sense, there was a genuine appreciation of my attempt.

I pursued a master's degree in Spanish Applied Linguistics and Second Language Acquisition to learn how to best teach second languages and how the brain works to learn them. I taught Spanish, for several years, and it still ranks up there as one of my favorite jobs. I love learning languages. I love how it allows me to get to know another group of people, new cultures, and new ways of life.

When I talk to students about their goals for their time abroad, they often say that one goal is to improve their language skills.

Since you are reading this chapter, I assume that one of your goals is to improve your language skills. Great! You're in luck, because I am about to bombard you with tips and strategies to help you improve. Some are conventional, and some are unconventional, but all will get you communicating and feeling more confident.

Even if you are a native English speaker and studying in an English-speaking country, you can still "learn the language." Believe me, as an American married to an English woman, I certainly needed help learning her language, in order for us to understand each other. The same idea exists if you are a native Spanish speaker from Mexico going to Argentina, for example; the language and vocabulary will differ enough for you to want to read on.

Language learning does not happen by osmosis. It takes effort. With these activities, however, it won't require as much effort as you think, and the benefits are tremendous.

THE BENEFITS

Yes, your language skills will improve, but what does that do for you? It helps you to meet new people, which will help you learn more about the culture and open your mind and your perspective, and if you're thinking about your career, it will open possibilities to work in other countries, or in your own country, with people who speak that language.

You're going to broaden your vocabulary, gain confidence, and increase proficiency in communication and comprehension; all of this will help to reduce the stress of not understanding the people around you.

Not to mention that your brain will actually grow by learning other languages. Neuroscience research shows that being bilingual improves executive function, keeps our brains healthier longer, delays the onset of diseases like Alzheimer's, increases problem-solving abilities, and filters out irrelevant information.[7]

And maybe best of all, you'll make a lot of people smile—happy that you are validating their identities and cultures—and give yourself the chance to meet so many new people.

"BUT RICH, I'M NOT A LANGUAGE LEARNER"

Maybe you are saying: "I'm just not a language learner. I've taken three years of X language, and I just can't learn it." Hopefully, after reading about the growth mindset, in Chapter 3, you no longer say that to yourself, but just in case, go back and reread that chapter to remember how much better it is to say to ourselves: "I haven't been able to learn French YET."

Think about it this way: if you've only studied the language in high school or college, you've basically been taught a language in order to pass a test or finish homework. For some people, that's enough motivation, but compare that to the motivation of being able to order food and drinks, meet new friends, tell your homestay what you like and don't like, or the

---

7   Mia Nacamulli, "The Benefits of a Bilingual Brain," TED.com, video 4:49, June 2015, https://www.youtube.com/watch?v=MMmOLN5zBLY.

awesome feeling of having a conversation about a topic you love, in a different language.

And don't worry, you're not going to be a "bad traveler" if you don't speak the language well. Suppose you make a genuine effort to learn some of the language. People around the world will truly appreciate it, and a simple *konnichiwa* (hello in Japanese) or *proseem* (please in Czech) might be the start of a relationship with someone you would not have met otherwise.

HOW TO BEST LEARN A LANGUAGE

Language learning is best accomplished when we have a desire to learn in order to *communicate*. We are social beings. Evolution shows us that we need to be social to survive. Being social means communicating, not taking tests.

What I'm trying to say is this: if you haven't learned much of the foreign language up until now, forget about that. This is a new start. Things can be different and better.

On the flip side, be realistic. If you are at an elementary level of German and studying in Berlin for three months, you will not become fluent. Fluent is a very strong word for me. You can definitely become much more proficient, and (especially if you are at a lower level) you have the opportunity to learn a great deal; but don't despair if you aren't reciting your own poetry—written in German—by the end of your program.

You don't have to do all of these activities to make gains, but I highly recommend you choose a few that will work for you and give it a go.

Quick note: when I say "target language" below, it means the language you are learning.

If you're ready, let's jump in.

SUGGESTIONS WITH THE HIGHEST IMPACT

→ Take a Language Class!

You did not need this book to tell you that taking a class will help you learn a language, but I want to reinforce that if you have the chance to take a language class, while abroad, DO IT! Again, you'll be learning content that you can **immediately use to communicate with people**. At a basic level, you'll learn food vocab that you can then use to order at a restaurant; at an intermediate level, you can actually start learning the past tense instead of just using the present tense and throwing your thumb over your shoulder to convey the past; and at an advanced level, you can debate whether soccer is or isn't the best sport in the world or whether there can ever be a truly democratic system of government.

→ Take a Class in the Target Language

If you have the opportunity and the confidence to take a class in the target language—meaning taking Art History in French or a History class in Japanese—you will get the double whammy of improving your language skills and learning about a specific topic that you are interested in. You might come out of every class with a headache, for the first couple of weeks, thinking you will never learn anything, but then the day will come when, without realizing it, you are taking notes in that language, thinking in that language, and then maybe even dreaming in that language.

→ Take a Third Language

If you really want a challenge, you can do what I did: take a third language in the country you are studying in. During my semester in Madrid, I took a Russian class at the local university. It was nearly impossible for me at first. I wanted to cry in there, because when I didn't understand the Russian, the teacher "helped me" by explaining it in Spanish. But eventually, I got through my tears and really enjoyed it. I'm sure I didn't learn as much Russian as I could have, but I met great friends, improved my Russian and Spanish, and relished the challenge.

➔》 FAST TRACK ACT: ATTEND OR SET UP A LANGUAGE EXCHANGE

In Spain, we call them *intercambios*—exchanges. You will improve your language and get so much more out of it. You'll find the opportunity to do many of the other things we talk about in this book: interview a local about their life; find out about their culture; get suggestions from them about things to do; and share your culture with them.

The way I've seen it work well before is: you meet up for a coffee, a walk, or a meal; you try to see different parts of the city; and you do half the time completely in one language and the other half completely in the other language, so you both get to practice listening and speaking. Be sure to have a notebook with you for some of the suggestions below.

If your program has not set up a language exchange (or conversation exchange, as they are sometimes called), try to set it up yourself. If you are at a local university, just ask around to see if anyone is interested or if they have an international office where they could set you up. Also, in many cities, restaurants or bars set up language exchanges, one night a week, where you can sit at the table with people speaking the language you are looking to practice; or you can help someone else practice.

If all else fails, I can pretty much guarantee that you'll find an app or a website that connects people trying to do an exchange, like MeetUp.com.

Everywhere I've ever done a language exchange like this, it has become one of my absolute favorite things about the whole experience abroad.

→ Interview a Local

This is similar to a language exchange but doesn't have to be as regular. This could be a one-off thing where you arrange to interview a local, in the target language, about a topic you are interested in. It could be for a class or just something you want to know more about. Setting up these interviews could be just the excuse you need to talk to someone. Often the hardest part of starting a conversation is starting the conversation. (Think about going to a party or a bar or a networking event where you don't know anyone.) By setting this up in advance, you don't have the awkwardness of trying to get it started.

You could do research beforehand, so you know more about the topic. For example, if you are interested in entrepreneurship, you could find entrepreneurs in that city who might be willing to talk to you.

→ Your Personal Address-Book Dictionary

Back in the day, my suggestion to students was to go abroad with a blank address book. For those too young to remember, people used to keep all of their contacts in a physical, paper address book, which was already in alphabetical order. I recommended that they carry it around with them, everywhere, and whenever they learned a new word—in class, from a street sign, from a friend, whatever—that they write it down in the book, which was already in alphabetical order; it became their own personal dictionary. Now, you can still do this, if you can find a paper address book (they are scarce), but it's possibly even better to use an online method. Both Apple and Google have "contacts" sections, which can serve the same purpose.

For example, if you have a Gmail address, you can use their "contacts" section. If you already use it for necessary contacts, all you have to do is start a new label called "French, Spanish, Italian," etc. Whenever you learn a new word, you put it in as the first name, and you put the translation in as the last name, and add it to the language label. Then you have yourself something that would look like this in Spanish:

Amar: To Love

Bailar: To Dance

Cocina: Kitchen

You can even print it out or export it to excel.

→ Good Old-Fashioned Vocab List

Just like the personal address-book dictionary, this requires you to hone your listening skills and be disciplined to write down what you learn. Instead of this being in alphabetical order, you would write this list down in the order that you hear the words or phrases. You can do this with a little notebook that you carry around or on a notepad on your phone. The benefit of doing it in a notebook is that, when you go to write it down, you're not distracted by new emails, messages, notifications, etc., which would take you away from what you were doing. The benefit of a notepad on your phone is that you will probably always have it with you, and you can easily access it there, on your computer, etc.

Maybe, make a SMART goal to learn ten words a day.

Then, to really help you learn the words: at the end of each day, reread the words that you have written that day; at the end of each week, reread all of the words from that week; at the end of each month, reread all of the words from that month.

The fun of this type of list is that you see a bunch of words and phrases, and it takes you back to that moment.

I once worked with a student who kept this type of list, and at the end of the semester, he had over 1,000 new vocab words. 1,000!

→ Food Vocab

Continuing with the vocab-list idea, one idea is to make a list of food vocabulary that includes the most common foods, idiomatic phrases that use food, menus in the target language, and tips for ordering.

→ There's More than One Way to Say "to Skin a Cat"

Once you start to grow your vocabulary, try to group it into categories. You don't have to sound like a Language-101 student forever; there are lots of ways to say "sad," for example: depressed, melancholic, teary, pained, unhappy, heartbroken, somber, pessimistic, etc.

You can add variety and nuance and expand your vocabulary with related words.

→ Play Taboo in the Target Language

You know that game Taboo where you have one word you are trying to get your team to say, but you can't say other related words, so you have to explain it in roundabout ways? That's the perfect practice for the real world abroad, where you end up doing a mix of Taboo and Charades and are trying to say "screwdriver," but you end up saying, "I need the thing that goes like this to push the things in...you know?"

→ Idioms and Slang

One of the most fun things to learn in other languages is slang. When we travel, we soon discover that people don't usually speak the way we learned in high-school language textbooks. It will certainly help you learn more vocab, but also help you understand more of what people are saying; when you get a good grasp of the slang and common idioms, you can name one section of your vocab list—or your contacts labels—"Slang."

→ Sticky Notes

The humble sticky note is not so humble when you realize its power to help you acquire a language. Here's the trick: when you learn a new word or phrase that you really want to start using, write it on a sticky note and put it somewhere in your housing where you will see it repeatedly—the bathroom mirror is a good place. That way, every time you are washing your hands or brushing your teeth, you remind yourself how to say it.

In the same manner, you can also look up words you want to learn and write them on these sticky notes. For beginners, learning how to say "Please," "Thank you," "Can I?" and "Where is…" is a good place to start, but you can use this at any level, to learn more advanced phrases.

Another use for the sticky note is to label things in your house to learn how to say them. Do you know how to say "table," "window," "mirror," or more advanced words like "blinds," "ceramic tiles," or "dishwasher"?

The cool thing about these sticky notes is that, once you have memorized/internalized the words or phrases, you replace them with new ones and keep the old sticky notes somewhere where you can go back to them to see how far you've come.

→ Writing in a Journal

As I was preparing to write this book, I went back to all of the journals I kept during my different study abroad experiences, as reminders of stories and lessons learned. Most of what I wrote was in English, but I did a lot of writing in Spanish, since I was at a higher level; I also used some basic Russian (that got better towards the end of my program) and Italian. It was such a good way to practice the language AND remember what I was doing and feeling during that time. My challenge to you: write a journal in the target language you are trying to learn! Even if you are writing at a child's level, every bit helps. But especially if you are at an intermediate level or higher, just try it. It will be hard, at first, but you'll see that you'll improve, and you'll be able to look back and see just how much. It's a great feeling.

→ Read Newspapers and Magazines in Other Languages

Depending on your level, you will most likely not understand everything you read, but that's okay, and it's not the point. The point is to get some more language input and pick up words where you can. Use the photos, headlines, and anything else for context. The bonus is that you will also learn more about the current events where you are studying. That will help you when you have conversations with the locals. If you actually have a newspaper or magazine in your hand, you can bring it to your next dinner with your homestay or meet up with a friend and ask them to explain something to you that you didn't quite get.

If you can, align the reading with personal interests. Like movies? Read magazines about movies. Sports fan? Plenty of local options to choose from.

→ Read Books in the Target Language

Depending on your level, you could pick up a regular book in the target language and give it a go. Even if you don't get every word, don't worry about it; it will be great practice as long as you understand enough of it.

If you have a lower level, find some "graded readers." These are actual books with stories, but they are written for students studying the language at different levels.

CHANGE YOUR COMPUTER AND PHONE SETTINGS TO THE TARGET LANGUAGE

By changing computer and phone settings to the target language, you will learn a whole new vocabulary, by repetition, and as I said above, the motivation is there because you are *using the language* for a purpose. Soon you'll start to think in the target language, without even noticing, and saying to yourself *enviar* (to send, in Spanish) or *ouvrir* (to open, in French).

WATCH MOVIES AND TV IN THE TARGET LANGUAGE AND/OR WITH SUBTITLES

Watching movies that you're familiar with in your native language will help you follow along when watching them in your target language. You can expand your vocabulary, while associating the images with new words. Movies are also good, because you'll become familiar with the conversational speech and not just the textbook speech you might be learning in class.

If you wouldn't understand anything by watching a show in the target language, you can watch it in your native language, with subtitles on in the target language. This works for both new shows that you haven't seen and some of your favorites that you know by heart.

Finally, watching the local TV shows in the local language can help you have something to share with a homestay or local roommate and has the bonus of cluing you into other cultural phenomena that we've talked about in this book. Watching the local news helps you keep up with current events in your city, country, and the world.

→ Listen to Local Radio Stations, Music, and Podcasts

The **local radio** station is a great way to pick up new vocab and phrases. Even listening to the weather forecasts, day after day, will teach you some basic but useful words.

These days you can find **music playlists** with music in every language, so find out what the most popular local bands are now (and were in the past) and listen to that music. In addition to helping you with the language, you might find music that you really like, and I guarantee that you will later associate that music with your time abroad, which is a great way of reminiscing.

There are **podcasts** about every interest these days, and many of them are in other languages. Find one or two that you are interested in and try to listen for just five or ten minutes a day, depending on your level.

→ Apps

It would be foolish to give you the names of specific language-learning apps here because they would be outdated by the time of publishing (except maybe Duolingo, recently valued at over $6 billion).[8]

→ Eavesdrop!

Our parents always told us that it is rude to eavesdrop, but I am now giving you permission. If you are sitting in a restaurant, on the bus, or at the market, focus on what people are saying around you and see what you can catch.

→ Language Pledge

Sign a language pledge, with your program, that says you will only speak the target language for the duration of the program. If that seems too daunting, do the language pledge for shorter periods at first. Start with ten minutes of only speaking the target language, then move up to one hour, one day, one week. Speak the target language even if you make mistakes, struggle to get words out, and feel like an infant. You are strengthening a muscle that needs time to grow.

→ Go to Religious Services in the Target Language

It doesn't matter if you are religious or not or if you are going to the services of your particular religion; you can go sit in religious services in the target language (if you are allowed) and try to pick up some of the language while getting an amazing cultural experience.

---

8   Echo Wang and Niket Nishant, "Duolingo Enters 'Major Leagues' with $6.5 Billion Valuation in Strong Debut," *Reuters*, July 28, 2021, https://www.reuters.com/technology/duolingo-valued-65-bln-shares-soar-debut-2021 -07-28/.

→ Take Tours in the Target Language

If you have the opportunity to take a tour in the target language, it's a great way to learn, because you are surrounded by the context of what you are learning. Like many of these suggestions, you may not get every word (you probably won't), but it's part of the learning process.

→ Language Fatigue

Speaking a second language 24/7 is exhausting, and just like when we exhaust any other muscle, we need a break. So push yourself to do these activities, but give yourself a break when you need it. Chill out with music, shows, podcasts, and talking to friends in your first language, for a while, then go back to the second language.

→ Make Mistakes

In my experience, the quickest language learners are the ones who are not afraid to make mistakes; they just speak. Whether they plan in their head first or not, they spit it out, and if it's wrong, they are not embarrassed; they see it as a learning opportunity (growth mindset). Remember my experience (a.k.a. mistake) of shouting at a young Russian woman and calling her a whore? (Wow; I really hope you read Chapter 3, so you can put that last sentence in its proper context!) I have never forgotten how to say juice in Russian, even though that was over twenty-five years ago. That massive mistake has solidified the language learning in my head.

So, be willing to make mistakes and even ask others to correct you, and you will improve more quickly, which will build your confidence, help you immerse yourself in the culture, and allow you to meet so many people you might not have met otherwise.

DIVE DEEPER INTO...

→ Language learning and effects on the brain:

Mia Nacamulli, "The Benefits of a Bilingual Brain," TED.com, video 4:49, June 2015, https://www.youtube.com/watch?v=MMmOLN5zBLY.

→ More tips to learning a language:

Lýdia Machová, "The Secrets of Learning a New Language," Ted.com, video 10:36, October 2022, https://www.ted.com/talks/lydia_machova _the_secrets_of_learning_a_new_language.

Chapter 9

SPEAKING IS NOT NECESSARILY COMMUNICATING

One of my Spanish coworkers from Barcelona, who speaks excellent English, was in the US on a study abroad recruiting road trip with three other twenty-something Americans, up and down the California coast. On one journey, from LA to San Francisco, she had to keep asking them to stop the car so she could go to the bathroom. She felt like she had to explain herself to them, so she said—in a very cute Spanish accent—"I am sorry, but the drinks are so big here, and I have a very small vagina."

She knew automatically, by their responses, that she had said something wrong. You see, bladder in Spanish is *vehiga,* which obviously sounds a bit like *vagina.*

SO THE QUESTION IS:

True or False: if you can speak another language, you can communicate well in that language?

If you are reading this book, you can understand English. Now, let's see if you can understand the next paragraph (and try reading it in an English woman's accent so you can sound like my wife, Kerry).

Kerry: Rich, stop faffing, get the nappy for Emma, and make sure Jack has clean pants. After I take the rubbish out, I'm going to make eggy bread for breakfast, so can you grab the Ketchup and salt? Remember, you are in charge of tea today and I've bought courgette and aubergine. We promised the kids a special pudding—maybe candy floss or jelly?

Me: Say what?

In case you didn't get some of that, let me translate from English to... English—or, better said: from British English to American English:

Kerry: Rich, stop (messing around), get the (diaper) for Emma, and make sure Jack has clean (underwear). After I take the (garbage) out, I'm going to make (French toast) for breakfast, so can you grab the Ketchup and salt? Remember you are in charge of (dinner) today and I've bought (zucchini) and (eggplant). We promised the kids a special (dessert)—maybe (cotton candy) or (Jell-O)?

Very important cultural note here—the British put Ketchup and salt on their French toast!! If there is one thing that I find hardest about crossing cultures, it's that French toast, universally, should NOT be eaten with Ketchup and salt; it must be maple syrup. I'm joking. Sort of.

Although my British wife and I are a small sample size, the constant misunderstandings between us (demonstrated above) indicate that the answer to that true-or-false question is a big fat "not necessarily."

There is much more to communication than understanding the words. So, even if you have already learned the language of the country you are going to (last chapter), or you already speak the language (this chapter) and you learn the nonverbal communication (next chapter), there is still room for miscommunication. Intercultural communication is so important that I'm dedicating three full chapters to it.

→ It's Like Learning Your First Language All Over Again

If you are studying in Australia, and someone says to you, "Mate, grab your thongs because we're heading to the beach this arvo. I reckon it could be a bit dodgy knowing some blokes were on the piss last night," it will help you to know that their *thongs* are flip-flops, *arvo* is afternoon, *dodgy* is shady, and *on the piss* means going out to get drunk.

As you can see, just because you already "speak the language" of the country you are studying in, doesn't mean you will understand everything. I recommend using the tips in the last chapter to learn this new vocab and save yourself from miscommunication.

The same would go for any heritage speaker of a language, studying in a country where they speak the same language, but differently, like a Mexican-American going to Chile, for example.

→ ACT: Start Your List

If you are studying in a country that speaks the same language as a language you already speak, research a list of what words might cause confusion. For example, in Britain, when you say "going to college," it doesn't mean the same as "university," whereas Americans use them almost interchangeably. You can easily find basic things like that on the internet.

It's not just the vocabulary that differs and makes communication difficult; it's also how people speak.

VERBAL GREETINGS

→ Hi, How Are You Doing?

Knowing how to greet someone across cultures can easily make us fit in or stick out. In the US, we greet people with a "Hi, how are you doing?" Do we really want to know how someone is doing? Not usually, but it's a pleasantry (another culturally charged word—it's pleasant to some, but not to others). That's why the answer doesn't usually go into a detailed analysis of our feelings.

A store clerk who greets with a "Hi, how are you today?" doesn't usually hear "Oh, wow, thanks for asking. I'm great ... well, actually I'm not. See, I think I may have just failed this exam that I really need to do well on, but I know I didn't study enough, because I've been having problems with my roommate ..."

Here's how this could play out across cultures: I was in London with a friend who likes his cigars, and we walked into a posh (expensive, swanky) cigar shop full of expensive leather armchairs. When we walked in, the older gentleman working there said "Good morning" to us in a typical/ stereotypical British upper-class, butler-like deadpan, no smile, and my friend chirped back in an American, "Good morning! How are you?" to which Jeeves responded (not sure if his name was Jeeves, but it seems appropriate), "Do you really want to know how I am feeling? Am I really supposed to answer that, or should we just carry on?"

To Jeeves, a cheery, smiley, in-your-face greeting is NOT what his typical customers are looking for. In fact, they would be entirely turned off by it.

On the surface (above the water), to someone from a "cheerful greeting culture," this would seem rude, but to his typical customers, if he greeted them with a big, toothy smile and "Hello! How ARE you today?!" it might seem intrusive or over-the-top.

> Please know that I am NOT saying that British people are all like this "Jeeves." I am saying that, in that cultural context of that posh cigar shop, it was "what we do around here, now."

When we greet someone in the US, and they ask how we are doing, we usually respond with a "Great!" or at least a "Good!"—something upbeat (and then, typically, something about being busy, but we've already covered that). If an American just says they are "good" without much excitement, it usually means they are bad because the default is an above-average jolliness.

I joke with my British friends because a typical greeting for them is: "You alright?" or if you ask how they are doing, the answer is "not bad," or "yeah, I'm alright," which is good! As in, the absence of bad is good enough.

And they joke with me because Americans are "too upbeat." How can we feel so great all the time?

ENGLISH AS A SECOND (OR THIRD, OR FOURTH) LANGUAGE
You may be studying in a country that either has English as an official second language or simply has a large English-speaking population; so if you go there, you will find yourself speaking English with people who

have it as a second (or third, or fourth) language. This means you have to change how you communicate, even in your first language.

Think of it from their perspective. Are you speaking too quickly? Are you using slang or jargon that they would not have learned in a classroom? What cultural references do you use that they wouldn't get?

CULTURE AND LANGUAGE INTERTWINED

Often without realizing it, we use a massive number of cultural references in our speech.

➔» FAST TRACK ACT: BASEBALL LINGO

Take three minutes to brainstorm a list of all of the everyday sayings or phrases used in English **that include baseball lingo**. For example, if I say, "Step up to the plate," I mean you need to be prepared; this is your time to make it happen. Ready? Go.

If you grew up in the US, where baseball is America's pastime and a huge part of American culture, you will have been able to come up with many phrases. If you grew up in a country that doesn't play baseball, you probably spent those last three minutes with a blank page in front of you.

Do you understand this paragraph?

Jessica, today, I need you to really *step up to the plate*. Go out there and *hit us a grand slam! Right off the bat*, they are gonna *throw you some curveballs* that *come out of left field*, but if you just give them a *ballpark figure*, it should be a *home run*. Let's *touch base* when you are done because I have another idea to *run past you*.

"Hey, Jim, *you're on deck!*"

Again, if baseball is a part of your heritage and culture, you would have gotten it all. On the other hand, when I show this to a group of students from all over the world, they look at me with blank stares, because they didn't get even 10 percent of it.

The point is that we can't try to communicate using cultural references when the other person doesn't get our cultural reference. The same goes for acronyms:

- ASAP—As soon as possible

- ETA—Estimated time of arrival

- CYA—Cover your ass

- WIIFM—What's in it for me?

- TLC—Tender, loving, care

- TBD—To be determined

→ ACT: Sports Language and Culture Intertwined

The next time you are with someone from the local culture, read them that baseball paragraph and ask them how much they understood. Then ask them to tell you words or common phrases that come from one of their country's sports.

FITTING IN OR STICKING OUT BECAUSE OF THE LANGUAGE

The British call it "banter," and the Australians call it "having a go," but most Americans call it "being mean."

The sarcasm or banter of the UK and Australia is almost an art form. It's a way of poking fun at your friends, in a playful and loving way, which is endearing in that culture but doesn't seem at all playful or loving when coming from a different cultural lens. The truth is, though, that if you are NOT getting made fun of, in one of those cultures, it's a BAD thing, because they do it to build connections. It's another example that shows we need to understand how verbal communication differs, in order to communicate properly.

When I get too used to the British way, I have to remind myself to tone it down with my American friends, or at least to say, "just kidding" (after poking fun at someone), so I don't offend.

As I've mentioned before, we don't even have to cross borders to learn these important lessons. African American Vernacular English (AAVE) is a linguistically proven way that some African Americans speak, with a different pronunciation and grammar than Standard American English (SAE). Although some people mistakenly say that it's an improper way of speaking, linguists agree that AAVE follows a set, systematic pattern that differs from Standard American English and is not incorrect; it "is systematic and rule-governed like all natural speech varieties."[9]

An example of AAVE would be: He don't know what he talkin' bout. Put that through an SAE filter, and it's "wrong," but the AAVE filter shows it follows exactly the right rules.

It would be like a British person saying that Americans speak improperly because American English differs from British English.

What's fascinating to me is that many people of color choose when to speak in AAVE and when to speak SAE. And guess how they choose? That's right; we just have to go back to our definitions of culture to see that people speak AAVE, in certain cultural contexts, when it is expected, reinforced, and rewarded—it's a way to fit in.

→ So Rude!

When we don't understand different communication patterns, the way others speak to us could come across as rude, and the way we speak could be interpreted as rude to others! Learning some basic communication frameworks will help you bridge some of these cultural communication gaps.

---

9   John R. Rickford, "LSA Resolution on the Oakland 'Ebonics' Issue," Linguistic Society of America, January 3, 1997, https://www.linguisticsociety.org/resource/lsa-resolution-oakland-ebonics-issue.

→ Formal vs. Informal

If you've ever studied a language, you have probably learned some sort of formal vs. informal conjugations of verbs like *Tú* or *Ud*, *Tu* or *vous*, *du* or *sie*, etc. Since we don't have that in English, this can be pretty confusing for students. Places like Spain rarely use the *Ud.*, or formal, pronoun, but other Spanish-speaking countries, like Mexico, use it often, and it's insulting to people to use the *tú* (informal) form of the verb. In fact, in Spain, if you speak to someone using the *Ud.* form, sometimes they get insulted because the *Ud.* form is reserved for much older people or someone in a high position of power.

Interestingly enough, even though we don't have different pronouns in English to separate formal vs. informal, our speech changes, when we want to be formal, by the words we use, the tone of voice, and even sentence structure. Imagine how hard *that is* for someone coming from outside the US to learn.

→ Swearing

Even swearing helps us fit in, stick out, or connect. The amount of swearing and the specific words we use (or don't use) help us fit in with certain cultural contexts.

Australians would say that they are more "potty mouths," compared to many Americans, because it's ok, or "normal."

Even within cultures in our own countries, I would bet that you swear more around your friends than during the holidays with your grandparents.

→ ACT: Reflection on Your Verbal Communication

In your time abroad, so far, have you had to change the way you communicate verbally? In what ways? How has it made you feel? Do any of your cultural-autopilot communication habits seem rude to the local culture? Does the way they communicate seem rude to you?

The hard part about having to change your communication style(s) is that, like so much else with culture, it is ingrained. We have to fight our initial instincts, just like with the math quiz in Chapter 3.

WHAT IS CONSIDERED LYING?

I was in the airport in Bangkok, Thailand, and I had a free first-class lounge pass from my US credit card. I was so excited, as I walked into this peaceful lounge, ready to spend my four-hour layover eating free food, drinking free drinks, observing cultural differences, and relaxing. I walked up to the desk, and the young Thai woman greeted me with a traditional Thai greeting of respect with palms pressed together on her chest, fingers pointing up, and a big smile. I said good morning and showed her my pass, eagerly asking if it would work for this lounge.

Her smile got bigger, she slightly nodded her head, and she softly said, "Yes, sir, that pass may work in another lounge."

Huh?

Me: So, can I go in here?

Her: *Big smile, nodding head, and just as softly:* Yes, sir, you can. It would be $110 US dollars.

Me: So, I can't use this pass?

Her: *Big smile, nodding head, traditional Thai version of hands clasped in front of chest:* Sir, maybe that pass will work at another lounge.

Me: Thank you. *Turn around. Walk out. Rejected and dejected.*

Why was she giving me "mixed messages" with her smiles and nodding? Why didn't she just tell me "No"? That would have saved me the time and energy to interpret what she was saying.

We have to look at it from her cultural point of view. In many Asian cultures, "saving face" is a strong value. That means not making the other person look bad, and maintaining an environment of harmony. In this case, saying "no" to me would make me look bad, because I should have known that a US-credit-card free pass would not work in a Thai airport. Deep down, I knew that, but I thought I would try, then got my hopes up with her smile and nod.

In my culture, a direct "no" or "no, sorry" would have been *better*. But, of course, I was not in my culture.

Some cultures are more direct in how they communicate (like the US), others are more indirect (like many countries in Asia or the Middle East), and others fit somewhere else on the scale.

When communicating across cultures, the differences can seem like lying. Just look at this semi tongue-in-cheek chart (similar to other widely-spread posts on the internet) of what the British say versus what they mean versus what others understand.

What the British say	What the British mean	What others understand
"That's not bad"	"That's quite good"	"It's bad"
"Very interesting"	"That is clearly nonsense"	"They are impressed!"
"With the greatest respect…"	"I think you are an idiot"	"They are listening to me"
"I'll bear it in mind"	"I've forgotten it already"	"They will probably do it"

Is a British person lying when they say something you've done is "very interesting" but they really mean it's not at all interesting? No, not at all. But if you don't understand how to interpret the way they speak and how to read between the lines, the situation is ripe for miscommunication.

By the way, Americans do this as well, but we call it "sugarcoating." It's when we have bad news to deliver, but we "coat it" in something positive (like bad-tasting medicine that has been coated in sugar).

In all of these examples, we see communication styles that could be misconstrued as lying if you are not from that culture and don't know the style.

→ Direct vs. Indirect: Just Get to the Point!

Another framework for looking at this is on a scale of direct to indirect communication. In cultures that are towards the direct end of the scale, people say what they mean, and they mean what they say. They also get straight to the point. The responsibility for effective communication is on the speaker.

In cultures that are towards the indirect end of the scale, they encourage listeners to read between the lines and might give a lot of background theory and "extra information" to get their point across. The responsibility is on the listener to effectively interpret the message.

When people from different ends of the spectrum come together to communicate, there could easily be misunderstood messages, but also confusion, frustration, anger, and accusations.

So if you find yourself frustrated with a communication-style difference that makes the speaker seem like they are lying, first try to understand why they are speaking the way they are and why you interpret it as lying. How is it different from the way you would have communicated?

This is easier said than done. I still sometimes get frustrated with the Spanish style of communication, when I expect an answer to be a quick yes or no or something short and to the point, but instead, it takes five minutes, and I still come away not having heard what I was expecting to hear. And they probably get frustrated with me if they feel I am not giving them enough of the background or story to help them understand what I truly mean.

~~~~~~

DO YOU HEAR WHAT I HEAR?

I was at a meeting, at a local university, where a Spanish colleague of mine asked a question to the Spanish host, which I thought should have resulted in a matter-of-fact, straight-up answer. Instead, she spoke for about five minutes, "dancing around the topic," talking about things that—to me—didn't matter. At the end, I still didn't feel like I understood a clear answer. Another American colleague of mine agreed. I mentioned that to my Spanish colleague, and he said, "No, I thought it was a great answer. She really gave me some good context surrounding why they do what they do."

~~~~~~

→ High Context vs. Low Context

Some cultures are considered low-context communicators, which means it's **what** is said that is important. That might seem obvious and normal to you if you come from a low-context culture (like the US), whereas other cultures are high context, meaning **how** something is said is most important.

~~~~~~

GET TO THE POINT!

One of my cultural-consulting clients was a German man coming to work in Spain. He was incredibly frustrated with Spanish people telling him so much of a story when he just needed a quick answer. He said, "If I can say something with fewer words, that's always better."

~~~~~~

Germany is one of the lowest-context cultures, where the how is not as important as the what. The point here, again, is not that one way of speaking is inherently better than another way, but in a particular cultural context, you will have more or less success depending on whether or not you can understand the communication styles.

→ Negative Feedback

When you have to give negative feedback, do you sugarcoat it? Do you do what we are taught to do in the US, which is give some positive feedback before giving the negative feedback? We don't even like the term "negative feedback"—we call it "constructive criticism."

NO SUGARCOATING

One of the French women I did a consulting job for had been working in the US for a couple of months when I did her training, and she told me she felt like she was rubbing people the wrong way when she'd go straight in and tell them that their performance was terrible. She would tell them that if they just improved X, they would come across much better. She had colleagues tell her she was too blunt, but there is no such thing as too blunt for her. Why would she have to say, "The way you supported your evidence was really strong, and your conclusion was solid, but if you don't mind, I think there is a way your introduction could be a little stronger"? She felt that was just muddying the issue and not clearly identifying what could be improved. The listener might not actually realize that something needed improving if she was not straight to the point.

→ ACT: Research Communication-Style Differences

Research how your own culture and the culture where you are studying communicate. I guarantee you will learn as much about your own style of communication as the others when you look into the different styles such as high-context vs. low-context, direct vs. indirect, emotionally expressive vs. emotionally unexpressive, and confrontational vs. non-confrontational. There are resources you can use in the *Dive Deeper Into...* section below.

→ Found in Translation

Deciphering intercultural communication is hard; there's no question about it. But it's incredibly important because so much can get lost in translation. There are books and books written about the topic because so many people struggle with it. I hope that, with some of the basic fundamentals, here, and with some of your own deeper research, your transition will be a little easier.

Plus, you'll gain some great skills to help you later in life as well. Your **active listening** will improve because you'll be more in tune with what successful communication looks like.

As you learn to see where the other person is coming from and why they speak the way that they do, you gain **empathy** because you better grasp their values and can be a more successful communicator.

You'll also learn more about your own communication styles, so you can communicate more effectively with people of different cultures.

This should help with all relationships, even romantic ones.

This is not just useful in everyday life, but also with work. Active listening and empathy are two skills that more and more employers are looking for when hiring. When you understand your own communication style better, you'll be more likely to sell yourself in a job interview, and you'll be a more effective team member and coworker.

But verbal communication is just part of the equation! And, in fact, it's a small part of intercultural communication. In the next chapter, we finish up by looking at the all-important nonverbal communication.

DIVE DEEPER INTO...

→ Intercultural communication:

Helen Spencer-Oatey and Peter Franklin, *Intercultural Interaction: A Multidisciplinary Approach to Intercultural Communication* (Basingstoke: Palgrave Macmillan. 2009).

Judith Martin and Thomas Nakayama, *Experiencing Intercultural Communication: An Introduction* (New York City: McGraw Hill Education, 2021).

→ African American vernacular English:

Langfocus, "AAVE—African American Vernacular English," YouTube 17:10, July 3, 2020, https://www.youtube.com/watch?v=UZpCdI6Z.

Chapter 10

THE MOST IMPORTANT GAME OF CHARADES YOU'LL EVER PLAY

ITALIAN GUY ON THE PHONE

In 2008, I traveled to Sicily for a vacation. Since I had interned abroad in Italy and studied the language years earlier, I could speak pretty well but not well enough to get my point across to the airlines who had lost my luggage, despite my best efforts over the phone. Luckily, I was staying at a little hostel where the guy working the front desk understood my plight and offered to use his phone to call the airline for me. He could tell that it was urgent to get my luggage right away because we would only be in that city for one more day before moving on.

He picks up the phone and calls the airline, starting with a pretty neutral voice, explaining the situation to them; but as the conversation goes on, I could tell he was getting frustrated with the lack of helpfulness of the person on the line. His voice was rising to the point where he was almost shouting, holding his phone to his ear with one hand and using the other hand for that Italian hand gesture meaning, "Come on! I can't believe you can't help me." Then he did something brilliant: he cradled the phone between his shoulder and his ear to hold it there and used BOTH HANDS to make the exasperated "COME ON!!" gesture that can't be done with just one hand! Obviously, the person on the other end of the call couldn't see him, but in the Italian guy's mind, he was better able to communicate when incorporating his innate nonverbal communication into the conversation—it's part of his communication process, seen or unseen. To him, this was his way to get his point across as to how frustrated he was!

Whatever he did worked, because I got my luggage back in time!

It was at that moment I thought: an Italian must have invented hands-free phone calls.

WHAT YOU SEE IS WHAT YOU GET

In this chapter, I give you the tools to better understand your own non-verbal style of communication; provide tips to help you observe other styles of communication and learn a bit of the why behind how others communicate; and teach you about some of the pitfalls you'll be able to avoid with this knowledge. I also want to help you learn from some of the massive mistakes I have made.

→ ACT: Yes, No

Try this activity with a friend: Friend A asks Friend B questions with "yes" or "no" answers. Friend B **answers truthfully**, by saying "yes" or "no," but does the **opposite** nonverbal communication of shaking their head for "no," when saying "yes," or nodding head for "yes" while saying "no."

Friend A should fire off at least five quick questions. Then switch roles. How did you do? Was that easy or hard? Why?

If you are like most people, it is not at all easy, and you end up dizzy because your head is sort of swirling around, in a circle, trying to do it properly. That's because our nonverbal communication habits end up ingrained and instinctual after so many years. Changing our nonverbal communication cues is hard because of how automatic they have become. Interpreting new cues is hard because we often lack the knowledge and awareness to understand their meaning.

→ Understanding Communication Styles

We are communicating ALL of the time. There are different studies and statistics, but the common idea is that **most** of our communication is **nonverbal**,[10] meaning that we are sending out messages, and others are interpreting those messages, even if we don't understand the words spoken. If that statistic is even close to true, it means we are sending hugely important signals about what we are trying to convey, *without saying a word*, because our gestures, facial expressions, and tone of voice communicate for us. The problem comes in when we misinterpret, or we are misinterpreted. The cues and rules for nonverbal communication change across cultures.

---

10   Albert Mehrabian, *Nonverbal Communication* (New Brunswick: Aldine Transaction, 1972).

Verbal communication is still important, as we saw in the last chapter, but understanding nonverbal communication styles—your own and the other's—is an important aspect of communicating when you start to swim in other cultural waters. This is so important that we're devoting this entire chapter to nonverbal communication.

→ Good News and Bad News

The good news for you, as you communicate across cultures, is that, without speaking a foreign language, you should be able to communicate with most of the world. The bad news is that if you don't understand the nonverbal communication you are encountering, you will miss a lot, or most likely, you will misinterpret what they mean to say and vice-versa.

Here's a quick example to give you an idea:

Anyone associated with the University of Texas at Austin is familiar with "hook 'em horns." It is a hand gesture where your thumb holds your middle and ring finger down while your index finger and pinky stick up, looking like bulls' horns. For the UT-Austin tribe, it's a greeting as common as waving and conveys friendship and connection.

Other people in the US use a similar hand gesture to mean rock and roll.

The problem is that the same hand gesture in Spain, Greece, or other countries of the Mediterranean means that your partner is cheating on you.

You can see the potential for miscommunication.

Nonverbal communication consists of not just gestures but also smiling, silence, body language, tone of voice, and other hidden clues that give out some idea of what people are trying to say.

Let's look at gestures first.

→ ACT: Gestures Your Culture Uses

Take as long as you need to write down all of the gestures that your culture uses to communicate something—that could be hand gestures or gestures with any part of your body—and then write down what they mean.

You probably wrote down about five to fifteen gestures if you haven't thought about this before. This is a little like the idea that, until we are out of our cultural waters, it's hard to look inwards and see what our culture is like. We use dozens, if not hundreds, of gestures, all of the time, to communicate, but we do it without thinking. Here are just a few from the US.

US GESTURES

- Middle finger
- Peace sign
- Smiling
- Winking
- Thumbs up
- A-OK
- Indicating that you want two of something
- Waving
- Raising your hand
- Nodding your head
- Shaking your head
- Patting someone on the head for a job well done
- Shrugging your shoulders
- Waving your hand in front of your nose, meaning something stinks
- Making a confused face
- Thinking/pondering
- Beckoning someone to come to you
- Shooing someone away
- Making eye contact
- Rubbing your fingers together to show money
- Raining cash with repetitive palm-swiping
- Flicking dust off your shoulder

- Rolling up your sleeves
- Putting your fists up
- Clapping
- Slow clapping

Here's the problem: with almost every single one of those examples, I can think of an example, from another culture, with the opposite meaning or an entirely different meaning. Here are a few:

In Britain, if you hold up two fingers—your pointer finger and your middle finger, palm facing you—to show that you want two of something, you are actually flicking someone off. This goes way back to when the English were at war with the French, and the main weapon for England was the bow and arrow. When an English soldier was captured, the French would chop off those two fingers so they couldn't shoot anymore. In turn, an Englishman who still had those two fingers would shove them up in the air, to basically say, "Up yours! I've still got my fingers."

In the Philippines, using one finger to beckon someone towards you is an insult, because that gesture is only used with a dog.

In Peru, waving your finger in front of your nose signifies that someone is rich and good-looking.

In Thailand, touching someone on the head is very insulting, because the head is considered sacred and the cleanest part of the body, so you don't want to dirty it with your hand.

→ ACT: Research, Observe, and Ask

Before traveling to a new country, it's a good idea to research their hand gestures and what they mean. Otherwise, you'll end up flicking someone off, in the UK, or saying that someone looks rich and handsome when you're really trying to say they stink.

I suggest you write down the gestures you have learned through research. Then ask a local to teach you some gestures. I can almost guarantee you that you will have learned some that they forgot to teach you because, again, it's like the fish in its own water—if they haven't had to reflect on this before, they are probably not aware of their nonverbal communication cues. This is a great excuse to meet some new people and to share your culture with them too.

Try using some of these gestures in conversation with locals. How does it feel to do it? Did it work? When they do work, it's a great feeling of accomplishment, even with the smallest of gestures.

Nonverbal communication goes way beyond hand gestures and body language and includes things that we do that we may have never been aware of.

→ Dress

What does the way a person dresses communicate about them? Do you wear the same outfit to church, class, work, or a dance club? I imagine the answer is no.

The reason that you dress differently, in those distinct scenarios, is that they are different cultures. The "going-out" culture is different from the "going to school" culture. And with certain groups of friends, you might feel more at ease dressing down and dressing comfortably, but with others, if you dressed like that, you might feel like you stick out.

Now imagine that amplified across country borders.

→ ACT: Iceberg Style of Dress

For this activity, you should go out and observe the way people dress.

How do they dress to go to school? To go shopping? Is it the same as what you see back home?

What are the colors like? Do people dress in brighter colors or muted tones? Or dark colors? Why do you think that is?

Do people dress formally or informally, and in what situations?

Do people dress conservatively or a bit more "risqué" (compared to your culture)? Do most people dress the same (relatively), or is there more individualism?

What do you think those observations of culture tell you about their values and beliefs?

Now, think about the way that you dress. What does that tell you about your values and beliefs? What would happen if you dressed the "wrong way" within a culture?

Some questions to think about with our style of dress and our values are:

- Is it more important to be comfortable or to look dressed up?

- Is social class important? Do we "prove" a socioeconomic class with the clothes or brands that we wear?

- What type of dress would be considered rude and make you not fit in?

For example, when I am back in the US, it still shocks me to see people wearing their sweaty workout clothes to the grocery store or out and about. That's something I almost never see in Spain, Italy, or France. A graduate-student friend, from the US, was working in Barcelona with me, and she signed up for a yoga class here. When she did what was normal back home—going to yoga and walking home from yoga in the same clothes—she felt extremely awkward. As she walked through the city, on her way home, she felt like she stuck out like a sore thumb because she was the only one in her workout clothes.

My students always comment that they feel underdressed in Barcelona, especially when going to class. They are used to going to class dressed down, even in sweatpants, flip flops, and old T-shirts. But they go to classes with local students in Europe, who are stylishly dressed.

→ ACT: American Style of Dress

Certain cultural tendencies are shared, across much of America, and others are regionally specific.

Step 1: How would you describe the way Americans dress where you are from, including shoes, tops, accessories, colors, etc.?

Step 2: What kinds of values might be expressed with those clothing choices?

→ ACT: Plan Your Packing

If you're reading this before you depart, I suggest you research what the dress is like where you're going, so you can do your best to feel comfortable and bring the right clothes with you. One woman I know says she uses Google Street View, to see how people are dressed, before she travels somewhere.

WHICH ONE OF THESE IS NOT LIKE THE OTHER?

I like to ask my students how they think their dress makes them stick out. Many Americans have a couple of telltale signs.

~~~~~~

YOU'RE NOT FROM AROUND HERE, ARE YOU?

I walked into a local clinic in a small town outside of Barcelona and wanted to find out who was the last in line. In Spain, since people are not often in a discernible line, you ask *"quién es el último"* ("who's last in line"), and you know you are next after that person.

But when I walked in, I went straight up to one guy and asked him, in English: "Are you waiting in line?" Lo and behold, he was from Indiana. He was wearing white socks, flip-flops, and an athletic tracksuit with a baseball hat on backward.

Needless to say, he stuck out. Of course, he would not have stuck out in Indiana, or many places in the US; in fact, in the US, I would have been the one who stuck out, with my jeans and "tight" (by US standards) button-down shirt, in the middle of a warm day. I have adapted my dress to fit in here, yet as soon as I go back to Chicago, I'm back in my shorts, T-shirts, and flip-flops.

~~~~~~

Do you have to dress exactly as the locals do? Of course, you don't—unless you are in a country where it is considered rude or forbidden to dress a certain way. For example, in Muslim countries, there are often rules for what women can and can't wear. But just like my grad student, above, or the example of my students at local universities, you might not want to feel like you stick out so much, every day, simply by the way you dress. It's good to be conscious of certain assumptions that will be made of us by the way we dress.

→ Eye Contact and Staring

What do you do when someone looks you in the eye? If it's a friend, a partner, or a family member, it's probably nice and comforting. But what if it's a stranger?

If it's someone who is trying to gain your trust, they might look you in the eye to prove that they are trustworthy and not "shifty-eyed." What if you are walking down the street, in a city you are not familiar with, and someone maintains steady eye contact? What if it's an unwavering look? How does that make you feel? What intentions are behind it? If you are in the US, it could feel threatening or simply weird and uncomfortable.

In both Italy and Spain, students have told me that they feel they get stared at more often, and it feels awkward to them. They don't feel comfortable, and they think, *What have I done wrong? Why are you staring at me?* In the US, especially, there is not much staring between strangers. In fact, if I am looking at someone and they lock eyes with me, I usually look away right away. However, it is "okay" to stare at people in both

Spain and Italy. I have learned that people in Italy like to see and be seen. It's considered "normal." Think of it this way: if they are dressing nice and trying to look fashionable, they don't mind if people are looking at them. In fact, one of my former colleagues once said to me that, if she is wearing a new outfit to the office and no one (male or female) says she looks *guapa* (good looking), she would be a little upset. Compare that to a US office environment, where you can go straight to the HR office if you say someone looks good-looking or nice!

→ ACT: Eye Contact and Staring

Write down what you've noticed about eye contact and staring where you are studying. How does it make you feel if it's different from where you come from?

→ Say Cheese—Smiling

When my friends from Europe travel to the US for at least a week, they always come back complaining that their cheeks hurt. At first, I was confused as to why that is, until they said it's because everyone is smiling at them, so they feel they have to smile back! This is something they are not used to. We Americans smile a lot compared to many other cultures in the world.

At first, when I studied in Russia, I thought that everyone was angry all the time. They didn't smile in the street or in a store or a restaurant, and when I met someone new, like my professors, they didn't smile either. I noticed that, even when Russians took photos, they don't say cheese (or the equivalent in Russian)—because they don't smile. Through my cultural lens, it looked like they were not having any fun in life. My first instinct was to think, *poor them; too bad they don't have more fun and are not happier like me.*

This is a classic example of two people looking at the same thing and interpreting it differently.

They look at me smiling all the time and think: *this guy is nuts, foolish, or hiding something.* In fact, there is a saying in Russian: "He who smiles the most is a fool." One of my American friends worked in Russia, and her Russian colleagues told her to stop smiling so much in restaurants, because it made her look stupid or artificial.

If you don't believe this or think it's exaggerated, look no further than the Russian government and media during the 2014 Winter Olympics in Sochi, Russia, which brought in millions of visitors from around the world. Russian media implored its citizens to smile more to make the international guests feel a little more welcome.[11]

What's going on here? Can I get an iceberg, please? Let's look deeper.

WHY DO AMERICANS SMILE SO MUCH?

Studies show that countries with high amounts of immigration tend to smile more, to show "the others" that they are friendly and aren't going to do harm. When they can't speak the same language, they communicate this peace offering through smiles. This historical tradition has carried on to today to convey a welcoming, friendly attitude and is almost obligatory because the absence of a smile in the US could mean the opposite: you are unfriendly and unwelcoming.

AND WHAT ABOUT THE RUSSIANS?

When Russia was the Soviet Union, people felt they could not trust people they didn't know. The KGB was spying on their own people, and outsiders were the enemy—not someone you would want to welcome in or give anything away to. And anti-American propaganda during the cold war suggested that Americans smiled when they were hiding something. Just like in the US, those historical roots carry on until today. I witnessed

---

11   Thomas Grove and Kazbeck Basayev, "Olympics-Smile! Russians Learn Hospitality before Sochi Games," *Reuters,* January 23, 2014, www.reuters.com/article/olympics-russia-hospitality-idUSL6N0JW39420140123.

Russian parents telling their children not to smile for photos. It would be hard to find Russians smiling at work, because work is a serious—not a fun—endeavor. But there were smiles and laughter aplenty within the home of my Russian homestay with their family and friends.

American students, especially females, need to be careful with this cultural difference wherever they are traveling. What is a "normal, friendly smile" in the US is often interpreted in other cultures as flirting and showing a type of romantic interest. You would be best served and safest to fight your natural instinct to smile and not concern yourself with feeling "mean" and "rude" for withholding smiles.

→ ACT: Reflection—Keep Track of How Much and When You Smile

In what situations are you smiling? Why are you smiling? What are you communicating when you smile? How does the other person—or people—interpret your smile?

→ Silence

This being a book, I can't do my favorite little trick from my workshops: after iceberging smiling, I just stop talking, and I count to eight in my head.

I stand pretty still, look around at the audience, and watch…them… squirm. Eight seconds of silence, and they get so uncomfortable—many of them smile, because they are uncomfortable and don't know what else to do. The students who were looking down look up after about three seconds of silence, to find out what is wrong.

What is going on? As a culture, **Americans don't do silence very well**.

Silence in the US communicates: awkwardness (a.k.a. "awkward silence"), discomfort, or a problem (a.k.a., he's getting the silent treatment).

Interrogators know that if they want someone to spill the beans, they can strategically stay silent, and the other person will often fill that silence by talking. When paired with some aggressive eye contact, it can be especially powerful and make someone squirm.

Interrogators will ask questions and be silent to get the suspect to talk and give away some bits of information, which they would rather do than suffer the silence.

→ ACT: See How Your Friends Do with Silence

The next time you are having a conversation with a friend, abruptly stop talking and count slowly to eight in your head, without letting on what you are doing. Pay attention to how the other person reacts. Did it feel uncomfortable for them? For you?

→ ACT: Comfort-Zone Challenge—Sit in Silence

My challenge to you is to try to get more comfortable with silence, and here's one way to practice:

Sit with a friend somewhere and stay silent, for five minutes, without looking at phones or any technology. How did it feel?

The reason it's helpful to become more comfortable with silence is that some cultures view silence as a sign of a true relationship. When two people can sit next to each other and not say anything, that is a great signal to the strength of their communication.

→ Stop Interrupting Me!

Silence can be a useful tool in cross-cultural communication. Small bits of silence help Americans know when it's their turn to talk. Americans are always taught not to interrupt people; we shouldn't start talking while someone else is talking; therefore, when we see— or hear—an opening in the conversation, that means we are allowed to jump in.

I have been in conversations with small groups of Spanish people where I can't get a word in, because where Americans don't like to interrupt, Spanish people are allowed to start talking even while the other person is talking. Spanish people are allowed to talk over each other. It's quite comical—and difficult at the same time—for me in a small group of Spanish people because I don't want to be "rude," so I don't start talking until there is a pause; and because they talk over each other, I never get a chance to jump in. It's another case of having to put aside what I consider rude to do what's right in that cultural context and just interrupt. To my amazement, over and over, they don't get upset or say, "Just let me finish," or "Don't interrupt me."

→ ACT: Observe Nonverbal Communication

Go to a bar, café, plaza, or park where you can observe lots of people from the local culture. Even if you are out of earshot, observe how they communicate nonverbally. Write down what you notice. Share your findings with your teachers, homestays, local friends, or other students, to get a deeper understanding of what you've observed.

→ The Emotional Scale and Tone of Voice

Some cultures are much more emotionally expressive when they talk, and they feel that injecting emotion into communication *enhances* it, whereas other cultures find that it *detracts*.

I come from a culture where showing passion and excitement is ok, but we should reserve raising voices and "yelling" for when something truly makes us angry.

IT'S NOT ANGER MANAGEMENT, IT'S JUST A DISCUSSION

I had a Spanish girlfriend for a while, but it didn't work out—partially because of communication issues. She was much more...how should I say it? Passionate in the way she spoke. She would raise her voice and shout, a lot more than I would, when she was excited or angry.

She explained to me that, because of her "Latin roots," when she is passionate about a topic, her voice raises, everyone involved gets more "heated," and that is part of the fun of the debate. It's boring to her to speak in an even-keel way; the more heated, the more exciting! Yet that "heat" makes people from other cultures (like me) feel uncomfortable and can lead to major cultural clashes.

We didn't last long. It was great for cultural investigation but not great for a relationship.

We can try to avoid some of that discomfort and miscommunication by preparing ourselves, observing, asking about the differences, and learning more about our own and other styles.

Now that you know how to communicate in your new surroundings, it's time to use that skill for something very important: eating and drinking! Food and drink are incredible lenses into your own culture and the one(s) you are now experiencing.

DIVE DEEPER INTO...

→ Nonverbal communication:

Judee K Burgoon, Valerie Manusov, and Laura K. Guerrero, *Nonverbal Communication* (New York City: Routledge, 2022).

Chapter 11

YOU ARE
HOW YOU EAT

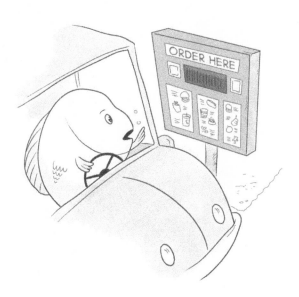

MY CULTURE SHOCK AT US RESTAURANTS

"Can I get you guys anything else?" the friendly waiter asked with a big smile. It was my first face-to-face get-together, in over a year, with my old college roommate—back in Chicago over pancakes and waffles at our favorite diner.

"No thanks, we're good."

"Ok, great; are you enjoying those pancakes?"

"Yep, they're delicious, thanks."

"Ok, guys, you enjoy, and just let me know if you need anything at all."

"Thanks."

Five minutes later, as we are getting into a juicy story, the waiter comes back and fills up our water classes, which are still half full. We stop our conversation.

"There you go, guys," says the cheery waiter.

Back into the conversation, a few minutes later, our server, "Sam" (we know this because he told us when he first came to our table), is back and leaves the check. "No rush here, fellas, just wanted to leave this here...unless you want anything else?"

I couldn't help but be frustrated by the constant interruptions, by the fact that our bill was sitting there in front of us—and all that it insinuated despite the *reassurance* that there was "no rush"—and that Sam couldn't just let us get on with it.

What was going on here?

Before I moved abroad, everything that happened there would have been "normal" to me; Sam would have been so friendly and polite, and I would have valued that enormously, but here I am getting frustrated and thinking, *Leave me alone, Sam! We will ask you if we need something, but until then, stay away.* My buddy didn't seem to mind as much.

It made me ask myself, what is **good customer service**, and can we iceberg that? Yes, of course we can!

This was a classic example for those wonderful questions: What is new to me? Why do they do that? Why do I do things the way I do them?

Food and drinks, to me, are two of the best prisms into learning about culture. So much so that we are dedicating two separate chapters to them.

We've always heard the refrain that you are what you eat, but I like to change that around to say **you are HOW you eat (and drink)**. We're going to do a deep dive into food, drink, and culture here, and I hope that you think about this, in ways that you never have before, and you learn to adapt to the new culture, through eating and drinking and learning more about yourself while we do it.

When teaching about food and culture, one of the things I love is that everyone eats, so everyone has experiences that we can iceberg. Also, many people travel because they enjoy eating foods from around the world, so it gives us the motivation to discover new cultures, appreciate them in new ways, and build relationships around the dinner table.

→ ACT: Your Own Food Survey

As we've seen, with other aspects of culture, it's best to start looking inward at ourselves first. Please take the time now to answer these questions about your own food habits.

1. What time do you typically start *and finish* these meals:

   a. Breakfast, Lunch, Dinner

2. What do you typically do while you are eating?

3. What three words would you use to describe food from your home country/region?

4. What three words would you use to describe the food of the country/region you are living in now?

5. How often do you eat a home-cooked meal vs. food made by someone else (at a restaurant, food to go, campus cafeteria, delivery)?

6. If you eat out at restaurants, what is your favorite sit-down restaurant back home?

    a. What is the decor like?

    b. Is it an extensive menu?

    c. Is it expensive?

    d. Do you tip?

    e. What else is happening at the restaurant besides sitting down and eating?

    f. How does this differ from restaurants you've eaten at in your new host country where you are studying?

7. How often do you eat "fast food?"

8. What kinds of food do you consume while walking on the street or driving in the car? How often?

9. Do you know many people who have ever tried a "fad diet"? Is it popular in your culture?

10. What are the foods you eat that connect you to your identity? How do you feel if you don't get to eat them while you are traveling?

11. What food-related challenges might you have if you moved permanently to another culture?

➔➔ FAST TRACK ACT: YOU ARE THE FOOD INTERVIEWER

Now that you've thought about these ideas, for yourself, it's time to find out more about the culture you are studying in. Take those same questions and find as many locals as you can survey and find out their answers.

When you complete this activity, you'll get a bonus from it because you:

- Think about your own food habits in a way that you probably haven't before.

- Start to see food patterns across cultures.

- Use food as a prism into the culture you are living in.

- Get to know someone from the local culture.

- Gain some practical tips about the city that you are living in.

- Get the chance to iceberg so many behaviors related to food.

Now we will break down the essence of those questions, to gain some valuable cultural insights.

SCHOOL MEALS AND LUNCHES

In Barcelona, I apologize to my Spanish coworkers when I eat lunch at my desk in twenty minutes, like I did at the office in Chicago, instead of eating with all of them in the lunchroom for forty-five minutes to an hour. Although I am fully aware that I am not doing something that is expected, rewarded, or reinforced in the culture, culture is so ingrained in us that some habits are hard to break. You may have heard a phrase similar to *You can take the boy out of Chicago, but you can't take Chicago out of the boy.* This habit of eating lunch quickly is something we are taught in the US from a very early age.

Chicken nuggets, sloppy joe, mac 'n' cheese, pizza squares, French fries. If reading this food list gives you nostalgia for your grade-school days, you are not alone. This is what I was served back then, and this is what many kids, aged six to ten, are still getting in their school cafeteria during their twenty—or thirty-minute lunch break.

That's why when I saw the menu for my kids' school lunch, I was floored. My kids are six and eight years old and go to public school in Barcelona. Here is an example of what they are eating this week:

	First Course	Second course	Dessert
Monday	Carrot-and-pumpkin soup	Egg-and-potato omelet	Yogurt
Tuesday	Lentil-and-sausage stew	Hake (fish) with salad	Apple
Wednesday	Macaroni with tomato sauce	Grilled chicken with salad	Seasonal fruit
Thursday	Spinach and potato	Beef-and-vegetable stew	Yogurt
Friday	Vegetable cream soup	Fried calamari with salad	Seasonal fruit

They can also choose from a vegetarian menu, a Halal menu, or a vegetarian-plus-no-lactose menu. These menus are chosen by a group made up of school administrators, registered nutritionists, parents, and even a representative from the mayor's office. Their goal is for the kids to start "good eating habits" (from their cultural lens) at a young age.

These good eating habits don't just include the food they eat; it includes how long they take to eat. The kids have one hour for their lunch, and they are served by staff who bring out their first course, then they wait until everyone finishes, get their second courses, wait for everyone to finish, and then get their desserts.

They sit down at small tables of six or eight kids, and they *learn to eat together.* This is something highly valued.

Also, they drink water only. There is no milk or juice or pop (my linguistic giveaway that I am from the Midwest—but you can say *soda* if you want.)

→ Iceberg School Lunches

What do you think are the values, beliefs, and perceptions behind each of the different ways of eating school lunch in the US and in Spain?

What we can interpret in the US is that the act of eating lunch isn't valued as highly as getting food into the kids and then getting them back to the classroom for learning, whereas, in Spain, *how* they eat is an important part of learning.

This is something that carries on, later in life, for Americans. When I ask students and adults about their lunch routines, I hear that they:

- Eat lunch in about twenty minutes.

- Eat something small and quick while they are doing something else like studying or working.

- Say lunch is not the most important meal of the day.

In addition to Spain, other countries find the act of eating a slow and healthy lunch so important that they start it at a very early age.

I highly recommend watching Michael Moore's documentary called *Where to Invade Next* where he shows the difference in school lunches between the US and France to drive this point home.

"THAT'S NOT EATING"

When I worked in Chicago, it was best to eat at your desk while you continued to work—that was the expected thing to do—because it showed a strong work ethic.

It was a shock when I went from that to when I started working in Barcelona. Almost every day at lunchtime, we shut down the office to go out for a *menú del día* which very much resembles the Spanish kids' lunch—but with alcohol and coffee. We had a first course, second course, dessert, a glass of wine, and a coffee. Between closing down our computers, walking to the restaurant, eating, walking home, and starting up again, over an hour had gone by.

We were starting to get more work, and one day, as my colleagues were heading out to lunch, I said, "Today, I am going to just get a *bocadillo* (sandwich) and eat while finishing up some work." The woman who was second-in-charge looked at me, very seriously, and said, "*Esto no es comer.*" ("That is not eating.")—meaning: okay, you can do that, but it is just putting food into your body and should not be considered the sacred act of eating. She probably pitied my thought that I could keep working, straight through, without taking a necessary break, and didn't get the social aspect of eating together. Both of those things are highly valued in Spanish culture. Many recent studies show that you should take breaks and not talk about work, in order to increase productivity![12]

12   Alan Kohll, "New Study Shows Correlation Between Employee Engagement and the Long-Lost Lunch Break," *Forbes*, May 29, 2018, www.forbes.com/sites/alankohll/2018/05/29/new-study-shows-correlation-between-employee-engagement-and-the-long-lost-lunch-break/?sh=2096cda34efc.

I THOUGHT I KNEW HEALTHY

What's the most important meal of the day to you? Growing up in the US, I was always taught that it was breakfast.

Is eating bread bad for you? So many fad diets (Atkins diet, South Beach, etc.) tell us that carbohydrates are the devil and should be eliminated or severely reduced.

Is eating dinner late at night going to make you gain weight?

Is using oil in your food really bad for you? Should we use butter? Margarine?

When I started traveling abroad, what I thought about food and food habits being healthy or not healthy was turned upside down.

Bread accompanies almost every meal in Spain—even if that meal is paella (a rice dish) and you've had *patatas bravas* (spicy, fried potatoes) as a starter. It's carb city!

In Italy, pasta is a staple of so many meals, and bread is usually there to accompany it.

Adapting to a new schedule of eating throws us off, because our bodies and minds are so used to eating at specific times of the day. Just look at these different schedules and meal sizes as approximations of when people eat meals in the US and Spain.

	USA	Spain
Breakfast	7:30 a.m. "Most important meal of the day"	8:00 a.m. Very light. Something small
Second breakfast	Doesn't exist	10:30 a.m. Slightly bigger
Lunch	12:00 p.m. Lighter and quick	2:00 p.m. Biggest meal of the day
Dinner	6:00 p.m. Bigger, heavier meal	9:00 p.m. Lighter meal

And finally, if I ever were to say a bad word about the almighty olive oil, in Spain or Italy, I would be ostracized. In the Mediterranean, olive oil is a cure-all. I've been to olive-oil tastings given by professionals with PhDs in Chemistry, who talk about the studies showing how olive oil is good for your heart, your liver, your skin, your digestion, and pretty much any ailment you might have!

So Spain and Italy must have higher obesity rates and lower life expectancy than the US, right? Wrong.

Obesity rates around the world, data from 2016.[13]

"Obesity is defined as having a body mass index (BMI) equal to or greater than thirty. BMI is a person's weight in kilograms, divided by his or her height in meters squared," yielding the percentages below.

United states	36.2%
Argentina	28.3%
Spain	23.8%
Italy	19.9%
China	6.2%
India	3.9%

Life-expectancy rates around the world, data from 2019.[14]

Spain	83.6 years
Italy	83.5 years
United States	78.9 years
China	76.9 years
Argentina	76.7 years
India	69.7 years

13 Hannah Ritchie and Max Roser, "Obesity," Our World in Data, 2017, ourworldindata.org/obesity#citation.

14 Mas Roser, Esteban Ortiz-Ospina, and Hannah Ritchie, "Life Expectancy," Our World in Data, October, 2019, ourworldindata.org/life-expectancy.

As we can see, obesity rates in Spain are 23.8 percent compared to 36.2 percent in the US. Life expectancy in Spain is 83.6 years compared to 78.9 years in the US. Of course, much more goes into these statistics than just food culture, but it goes to show that everything I learned was "the healthy way to eat" maybe wasn't.

It further illustrates the point made back in Chapter 2—once we've seen something one way, for so long, it's hard to see it from a different perspective. It's a challenge for many US students to have long lunches that last for an hour to two hours and to eat dinner with their homestay parents at 9:30 p.m. Not only is it hard, but it also seems wrong—at first. Then a funny thing happens, and after a while, they learn that they actually kind of like doing it the other way, or at least they accept it and adapt to it. This is a good step in becoming that cultural chameleon that shifts behaviors depending on the cultural context that it is in. Being able to see things from the other perspective, and to live it, adapt to it, or even assimilate it into our own behaviors is an impressive skill.

GROCERY SHOPPING: ICEBERGED

My biggest food shock, when I go back to the US after living abroad for so long, comes from grocery shopping. Here's what jumps out to me:

- The size of the shopping carts. I can fit three Spanish shopping carts into one shopping cart back in the US.

- The size of the food itself! Giant bags of chips, giant boxes of cereal, giant bags of chocolate. Especially if you are going to a Costco or a grocery store like that.

- The variety and the choice in almost every category. One look at the cereal aisle of a large grocery store gives you the idea. Also, if I want to buy salad dressing, not only do I have the choice of Ranch, Blue cheese, Honey Mustard, Vinaigrette, Thousand Island, and more, but within each of those categories, there are more categories. Hidden Valley, one of the many brands of Ranch dressing, boasts these options:

- Jalapeño Bacon Ranch

- Cheddar and Bacon Flavored Ranch

- Cilantro Lime Ranch

- Buffalo Ranch

- Dairy Free

- It's not just ranch dressing; look at the variety with mustards, ketchups, hot sauces, breads, etc.

- So much preprepared food and ready-to-eat straight out of the package—even apples that are already sliced into bite-size pieces and ready to be eaten eat as soon as you open the bag.

- People drive to the grocery store.

- People go grocery shopping in their gym clothes—either right before the gym or right after the gym—without showering and changing into clean clothes.

- People use coupons.

- How well the US can advertise and sell. Everything seems to be on sale: buy one get one free salsa when you buy chips, all of the special packaging that appeals to different customer segments, etc.

- There are smiling staff, ready to help you find whatever you need.

- Each aisle is numbered and labeled with exactly what you'll find.

- The child-friendly food is placed lower, so it's at eye level for kids.

- The ability to buy so many different items in a grocery store—not just food and drink.

→ Deep Dive: Grocery Cultural Waters

So many of the things I wrote above may seem normal to you to the point that you say, "So what? Why do you even mention it?" But from my travels around the world, every single thing I wrote is something that sticks out to me as unique and different from what I've seen in other places, and more interestingly, everything can be iceberged.

> Let's stop for a minute here. Are you starting to feel defensive about your food culture? I often find that when I am abroad, I am defensive about US culture, and when I am in the US, I am defending other cultures. If so, that's normal, and a great indication that this giant cultural mirror we are holding up is working to help you reflect more on your own culture and see things from a different perspective. Sometimes it's hard to hear, and it's easy to get defensive. Recognizing this feeling and working through it are both important exercises. My comments here are not judgments, just observations and comparisons that I find fascinating to iceberg. This is also a good time for a reminder about what I said before—that not everything that happens to be common in a country is common everywhere within its borders. For example, food shopping in big cities within the US is often quite different from how it is in rural towns and villages.

We could take countless pages to continue to iceberg every single thing up there, but I'm just going to take a couple for now (even though I'm dying to do it with all of them, because I love this topic!).

Grocery shopping with my wife, Kerry, and son, Jack, when we first moved to Fort Collins, Colorado, for three months in 2014.

People drive to the grocery store, and the grocery carts are huge. People buy a lot of food, enough to last them at least a week, and maybe two weeks. They save time and don't have to go back to the store for as long as possible. They drive so they can load up the car with groceries, which is why the cart is so big. One value is saving money through quantity, and another value is saving time.

Compare that to grocery shopping in several European cities that I have lived in and where I live now: first of all, I haven't owned a car in the twenty years that I've lived in Barcelona, so I always walk to the grocery store. The trolley shopping carts are about a third of the size of the cart that I used when I was in the US. And I usually don't even grab a trolley cart; I take a handheld basket or a pulley basket because I'm only buying enough food to last for three to four days, then I have to walk home with it all in my arms. Sometimes, when we shop for more food, we bring our *carrito* with us—picture an upright bag on wheels that keeps its shape, which you can fill with food.

Many people over here also do their shopping at an open-air market where there are several stalls, each specializing in something different. So you go wait in line at one place for your vegetables, another one for your cheese and eggs, another for your meat, and another for your fish.

People who do their shopping like that value the fresh quality of the food over the quantity and the time they would save at a one-stop shop. They also value knowing the person at the market and trusting their opinion on, for example, the best poultry to get that day.

Next, let's take the ready-to-go **sliced apples** in the packet and iceberg that. The value we see there, once again, is convenience. A good friend of mine, who lives outside of Chicago, works full time—as does her husband—and has two young kids. Time is precious to them, so having to wash an apple, slice it up, and find the right container for it, making sure it won't turn brown in the next few hours, is much less appealing and convenient than grabbing the bag of pre-sliced, prewashed apples out of the fridge and getting a move on. The perfect solution!

You can find thousands of other "food items of convenience," but some others that stuck out to me were: a bread machine mix you just throw in (instead of finding the individual ingredients), microwave popcorn (instead of popping kernels on the stove), mac 'n' cheese in a box, Campbell's soup varieties in a can, ready-made (versus making homemade soups).

Finally, let's look at all of the options. Choice! So much choice everywhere. All of this choice allows people to get exactly what they are looking for (individualism), but it also allows their creativity to flow. Americans value creativity and ingenuity. If you look at the Ranch website, they know about American values, so they provide tons of options for recipes and tips on how to use all of their products. That means we can take what would be the typical option and jazz it up how we want it.

That creativity gives us the chance for "new and improved," which is valued in the US.

→ ACT: Go Grocery Shopping

One of the first things that I do when I travel to a new country is go grocery shopping. I love to see the new flavors, smells, food varieties, and how people shop. For example, in the pasta aisle in Italy, it's mind-blowing to see how many different shapes of pasta they have—about 400 by some counts.[15]

You will go grocery shopping anyway, but now you can do it with a new lens and a new power of observation.

What are the cultural differences that stick out to you? What do you observe, and what can that tell you about their culture? How does it compare to the way you shop back home?

Also, if there are open-air markets, do some shopping there. The great thing about this is that you have to interact with people, to get what you want, instead of silently walking through a store choosing what you want on your own.

I find it especially fun to check out different flavors of potato chips in different countries. Some of my personal favorites:

- Banana-yogurt-shrimp flavor in Singapore

- Caviar flavor in Russia

- Roasted-chicken flavor in Spain

---

15 "Regional Guide to Pasta from North to South," Eataly, accessed February 6, 2022, www.eataly.com/us_en/
    magazine/how-to/italian-pasta-guide/.

→ Bonus ACT:

Taste the "strangest" flavored potato chips wherever you are studying! Play a game with your friends where you get several different flavors, put them in bowls without the bags, and people have to eat them and guess what the flavor is.

EATING AT RESTAURANTS: ICEBERGED

Analyzing eating at restaurants gives us a beautiful prism into cultural differences. When I am back in the US, I love going out to eat but can't help but feel the culture shock.

One key difference is the idea that "the customer is always right," which is very American. Giving the customer what they want is certainly not always shared in all other countries. I have definitely been to restaurants around the world where, as a customer, I was made to feel like the restaurant was doing me a favor. I couldn't imagine that in the US.

Another difference, as I mentioned at the start of this chapter, is the super-friendly, smiling servers. They are not what I'm used to, living in Europe. If you come from the US, you might be thinking, *But it is so much better to have a smiling waiter than an unsmiling, grouchy waiter!* If that's what you're saying in your head, that's fantastic cultural material right there. It bears repeating that I am not usually saying that one way of doing things is, universally, better than another way. I'm saying that there is a better way of doing things *within that cultural context.*

An unsmiling and unfriendly waiter in the Midwest of the US would not do well, whereas that same waiter around the world would not have any problems at all. It's about what that cultural context expects, reinforces, and rewards.

Travelers from the US to Spain often have trouble adapting to the customer service here, at first, because they feel like servers are rude to them. They see how the waiters don't rock up to the table with a smile, don't tell them where they are from, don't come back to the table to check on them, and don't offer them free refills of water (water is not free here; in fact, it usually costs more than wine). They don't push you to buy the most expensive thing on the menu, they don't have tips and tricks to get you to buy dessert, and they don't bring the bill until you ask for it. They also don't say, "Hi! My name is So-and-so, and my favorite meal here is the sticky ribs made with our own special recipe sauce, which comes with a side of bacon-covered au gratin potatoes."

All of this from the cultural lens of US "good customer service" means they've failed. However, there are many good reasons that all of this is "good customer service" to a Spanish cultural lens:

A Spanish person hasn't come to the restaurant to be friends with the waiter; they've come to spend quality time with the people they are with, and that usually means being able to order their food and drinks and then get on with their conversations with as few interruptions as possible. They will flag down the waiter to ask for something instead of getting interrupted on the off chance they might want something more.

TIPPING

And all this culminates with the huge cultural difference of tipping.

In the US, tipping is the norm in many different situations: restaurants, hairdressers, taxis, valets, bartenders, and the person who makes your coffee. It's customary to leave 15–20 percent, on top of the bill, at a restaurant, and, in fact, many restaurants are now automatically adding a 20 percent tip to the bill.

As with other cultural differences in this book, I cannot give you the exact tipping suggestion for your country, because that varies. It might be similar to the US, or it might even be considered an insult to leave a tip. What I want you to think about is the *why* behind the action. What are the values and beliefs that drive the tipping behavior? What is expected, reinforced, and rewarded?

I have an American friend who comes over to Spain and still leaves big tips because he thinks: *Wouldn't that server who worked on our table RATHER get a big tip? Doesn't everyone want a big tip?*

From a US cultural lens, it makes a lot of sense to give a big tip for a job well done. Why?

The US values hard work and productivity; they value friendliness, and they are individualistic, so hard work = more money. Knowing the national culture of the US, we understand that a server makes the minimum of minimum wages for that type of job, which is currently around $2.00 an hour. They basically live off of tips.

In other cultures, working hard and being productive is important, but it's not the most important thing. A waiter doesn't have to be friendly; they have to get their job done, which means bringing the right food and drinks to the customers. Some countries pride themselves on paying a living wage to servers; they don't expect a tip on top of their salary. The restaurant has already built that money into the price of the food.

Also, in many restaurants around the world, the tip doesn't just go to the server serving you. When you leave a tip, it goes into the pot that gets split between all of the people who helped get the food from the kitchen to your table. It's a collective tip, not an individual one.

If people from 15–20 percent tipping cultures start going to non- or small-tipping cultures and leaving huge tips, they could change the local culture. Local people do not want foreigners coming in with their tipping, because that might mean that THEY would start to be expected to leave bigger tips, too, and that's "not what they do around here, now."

→ ACT: Cultural Differences at Restaurants Where You Are Studying

What are the differences you've noticed when you go to restaurants in your host city? Is the customer service the same as in the US? Are you supposed to tip? If so, how much and why? Ask a local what the values and beliefs behind tipping are. Also, ask a server what they think about tipping.

DO WE HAVE A WORD FOR THAT?

What do we call that time, after lunch or dinner is over, that we spend talking with the people we shared the meal with?

This question stumps my American students, every time, because we don't have a word for it. But Spanish people do; it's called the *sobremesa*. This literally refers to the time after lunch or dinner when you end up talking—sometimes for hours. This is my favorite time of the day. There is nothing better than a paella lunch, on the beach with my friends, that starts at 2:00 p.m. and ends at 5:00 or 6:00 p.m. The *sobremesa* is a fantastic cultural gem that truly combines several Spanish values: building relationships; taking time for friends; and living more for the moment.

Reflection: Does something like the *sobremesa* exist where you are studying? Is it something you are used to, getting used to, or having difficulty adjusting to?

I WANT IT MY WAY

The last time I was back in the states, I went out to dinner with five of my friends, and this stuck out to me: one of my friends ordered the chicken parmesan, but with gluten-free bread crumbs and the sauce on the side; another ordered the salmon with a side salad, but hold the onions; another ordered the house burger, medium-rare with extra grilled onions and jalapeños; and I was just planning on ordering my meal as it came, like I do here in Spain, but I had to choose the bread, the sides, and the salad dressings (in Spain there is usually one choice of salad dressing—oil and vinegar) and then "a beer" at which time the waiter handed me a craft-beer menu with about twenty choices. It was an incredible display of individualism in food. The identity of "I," their personal identity, shines in this example.

Compare that to my last meal out in Barcelona, when everyone ordered what was listed on the menu and the waiter did not have to ask any questions nor did we have to give any further choice or explanation.

We Americans love variety and choice so we can personalize our… everything, even food. Look at this photo I took at a diner in the US. I asked the server if they had hot sauce, and she pointed me in this direction.

And think about going to Chipotle or Subway and all of the options you have there. Think about buffets and all of the options you have. These restaurants are playing to American values of individualism—making the food the way WE want it (as in Subway's slogan at one point, "Have it your way," or Burger King's "Your way"). They also play to our values of creativity and improvement—take an existing meal and make it your own to "improve it."

If we are how we eat, let's continue looking into how the way we eat out at restaurants tells us something about ourselves.

THE CHEESECAKE FACTORY IS AMERICA IN A RESTAURANT

If you've ever been to The Cheesecake Factory restaurant, you've seen that reading their menu is like reading a novel. Interestingly enough, in 2018, their CEO decided to cap their menu at 250 items. 250!! And the portion sizes are enormous. Americans really value quantity.

"Growing up, my parents used to go down to Miami and gush about the large portions they commonly saw down there," Overton (CEO of The Cheesecake Factory) said. "So right away, I knew it was important for us to have large portions. Again, I didn't have restaurant experience, but it just seemed like the right thing to do for our business."[16]

"The *excess*, the *variety*, and the *overall scatterbrained melting pot of the menu* are why people love and continue to go to the Cheesecake Factory!" (emphasis added)

Overton said, *"We work incredibly hard*, and we try to give people what they want, and what they love. *We have something for everyone.* And that's why I think we've been so successful." (emphasis added)

In the interview with the CEO, we hear American values over and over: excess (quantity = value for money), variety, diversity of choice, and working hard and giving the customer what they want.

---

16 Wil Fulton, "Why Cheesecake Factory's Menu is so Damn Big, According to its Founder," Thrillist, October 19, 2018, www.thrillist.com/eat/nation/cheesecake-factory-menu-explained.

All of that choice can be great, for a culture that likes it, but can be so overwhelming for one that's not used to it.

YOU ARE HOW YOU EAT

"I'll tell you what I like about Chinese people. They're hanging in there with the chopsticks, aren't they? You know they've seen the fork. They're staying with the sticks. I don't know how they missed it. Chinese farmer gets up, works in the field with a shovel all day. Shovel. Spoon. Come on. You're not plowing forty acres with a couple of pool cues!"
—Jerry Seinfeld

Jerry Seinfeld is humorously poking fun at how Chinese people "still eat" with chopsticks, even though they've seen the fork and knife, insinuating that eating with a fork and a knife is better. Of course, this is a joke, which somewhat limits our cultural analysis, but he is looking at it with his American cultural lens. Chinese people have, of course, seen a fork and a knife, but in their eyes, it's not better to eat that way. This is a perfect example of two people seeing the same thing but interpreting it very differently. In fact, a Chinese student in the US told me, "I prefer using chopsticks even for most American food. It's just easier."

→ ACT: Reflection

Do you eat with your hands? With a fork and knife? With chopsticks? What does that say about you?

The question is, how well will you adapt when another culture eats a different way? Will you not only learn how to eat properly in that culture, but will you also understand the why behind it?

→ ACT: Eat "Weird Stuff"

Get out of your comfort zone and eat some "weird stuff." Eat as the locals do. If you are struggling, just think of it this way: they are "thank-you bites and bragging rights." If someone offers you something that looks strange, try a little and say, "Thank you." If it's something especially different, think of the great stories you'll be able to tell your friends—bragging rights.

FOOD AS CULTURE SHOCK

When we take our students to Morocco, and they get to stay with homestay families there, they often see how the families put a large bowl of couscous, vegetables, and meat in the center of a big table, and everyone starts to dig in … literally dig in with their hands, to grab the food, put it in their mouth, and then go in for more. When I stayed with one of these families, I commented that in the US we each serve ourselves, on our own plates, then use our knives, forks, or spoons to eat. They responded with something that has always stuck with me: "What a shame that you don't get the pure taste of the food, directly, because it's been on a metal utensil. Food tastes best when you eat with your hands like it was meant to be." It also seemed a little "cold" to them to eat individually and not share the food together with your hands going into a communal pot.

The idea of communal vs. individual can be seen in how we eat out at restaurants in the US versus going out for tapas in Spain, for example. Tapas are small plates of food meant to be shared among several people. When we go out to get tapas, we have to decide, as a group, what to get and negotiate, so that everyone gets something they want. There is give-and-take. The shared eating style can be seen in countries like China (hot pot), Morocco as we just saw, Ethiopia (eating off of the injera bread), and many more.

Learning to adapt to other cultures' food habits is a great way to build cross-cultural agility skills. It can also be the way to get the comfort you need on a particularly difficult day. There is nothing like biting into your favorite comfort foods to give you a delicious taste of home.

→ ACT: Do a Cooking Class!

How is this for homework: find a way to do a cooking class in the place you are studying. This has always been one of my favorite things to do, when I travel, because I get to eat delicious food, find out the local way of eating, and usually meet some locals. If you can't afford to do an official class, but you live with a homestay or local roommates, ask them to teach you to cook some staple foods.

What have you learned about how people eat in your new host culture, and what does it tell you about their values and beliefs?

Now that you've learned how to eat in another country, you're halfway there; but there's still a whole cultural world behind how people drink.

DIVE DEEPER INTO...

→ School lunch differences between the US and France:

Michael Moore, "School Lunch France," February 3, 2017, YouTube video 6:41, www.youtube.com/watch?v=rXK591Rp4BU.

→ Learning about the world through food:

Most books by the author Mark Kurlansky.

→ Food and culture around the world:

Most books and resources by the late author Anthony Bourdain.

Chapter 12

RAISE A GLASS

IT'S 5 O'CLOCK SOMEWHERE

I went for a coffee near my house outside Barcelona at 10:00 a.m. on a Thursday. I counted three different tables (out of nine) where people were drinking alcohol. This was a typical Thursday—not a special holiday in any way.

I was in the US, and I had the chance to meet a group of people from a small town of 1,000 inhabitants an hour north of Chicago. One of the women I met runs a diner. This entire town was dry (no alcohol allowed) until 2018, so I remarked how it must be nice to be able to finally sell alcohol. She said, "Oh no; we are only open for breakfast and lunch, and I run a family diner; we will not be serving alcoholic beverages, **because I don't think it's right in a family restaurant**. If people want alcohol, they can go to the pub, at night, or buy it from the gas station down the road."

By now, your iceberging muscles must be tingling with excitement. Don't worry; we will get to that later in the chapter, but first ...

How do you drink?

→ ACT: And Now Your Own Drink Survey

As we saw with the food survey, we can glean so much cultural information, about ourselves and others, through food, but you're about to see that just as much can come from drinks too. Answer the following questions:

1. What kinds of drinks do you consume while walking on the street or driving in the car? How often?

2. Hot drinks

   a. Do you drink any hot drinks? Which ones?

   b. Do you drink coffee? If so, what is your favorite coffee drink?

   c. Do you drink tea? How do you take your tea?

   d. How many hot drinks do you drink per day?

   e. Where are you when you are drinking these drinks? (i.e., at a café, at home, in the car, walking on the street)

   f. Are you usually on your own while drinking them or with someone else?

3. Alcohol

   a. Do you drink alcohol?

   b. At what time of day do you typically drink alcohol?

   c. How many drinks do you consume at one sitting?

   d. What type(s) of alcohol do you consume?

   e. Do you always, sometimes, or never eat food while drinking?

   f. Does drinking alcohol ever become competitive in your social group (i.e., who can drink the most or the fastest)?

   g. How old were you when you started to drink alcohol?

   h. Is there an age where you are allowed to drink alcohol in your home country? What age is it?

   i. Do you think people in your culture drink too much?

4. What drink-related challenges might you have if you moved permanently to another culture?

FAST TRACK ACT:
YOU ARE THE DRINK INTERVIEWER

Use these questions above to survey as many locals as possible, then compare your answers to theirs. What interesting similarities or differences did you find?

HOT DRINKS

Let's get warmed up by iceberging coffee drinking habits around the world.

→ ACT: Iceberging Coffee Drinking in the US

Step 1: Describe coffee drinking in the US. What words would you use to describe it above the water? What are the observable behaviors? Take a few minutes and write that down—and remember that all of this is a description above the water—without analyzing anything yet.

Step 2: If you look at the behaviors in Step 1 and dive deep under the water to understand the values, beliefs, and perceptions behind those behaviors, what can you find?

Here are some of the answers I get from my students for Steps 1 and 2:

• People get coffee to go.

  ◦ Values:

- Multitasking and productivity. Drinking coffee while doing other things.

- Advertising. When we get coffee to go, we are doing the advertising for the coffee company, with the cups and the cupholders, which have their logos on them.

- The sizes are big (note: "big" is a relative term used when compared to something else).

  - Value: Quantity as a value for money. The more, the better.

- People drink a lot of coffee (note: "a lot" is a relative term used when compared to something else).

  - Value: Coffee gives us the caffeine kick to keep moving and keep being productive.

- They often get coffee from a drive-through.

  - Value: Convenience, multitasking.

- The coffee is usually not just coffee: it's got flavors, sugar, different types of milk, whipped cream.

  - Value: Choice, options, having it the way we want it to be, having it personalized to us, quantity over quality (of the coffee flavor itself).

- There are specialty coffees at different times of the year (like pumpkin spice at Halloween or peppermint at Christmas time).

- Value: Marketing, variety.

- If you go into a place to buy coffee, they often ask your name so they can write it on the cup.

  - Value: Personalized branding, as in you can order a drink that is specific to you.

- If you actually go to a café and drink the coffee there, it's usually with your laptop so you can study.

  - Value: Multitasking, working, productivity.

- They often try to sell you something else as well: a variety of baked goods and souvenirs.

  - Value: marketing, consuming, maybe belonging if you buy something with a logo that shows you belong to the culture of those who go to that café.

WHAT STARBUCKS CAN TELL US ABOUT VALUES

Go into any Starbucks, and you'll probably see two kinds of tables: round tables and rectangular tables. There's a reason for the round tables. According to *Reader's Digest*, the round tables are supposed to *make you feel more at home when you're by yourself.*[17] (emphasis added)

---

17 Jessica Booth, "15 Things You Never Knew about Starbucks," Insider, July 20, 2018, https://www.insider.com/starbucks-fun-facts-2018-7#theres-a-reason-for-the-round-tables-in-the-restaurants-7.

Let's pause here so the idea of "feeling at home by yourself"—probably while working—sinks in. You'll see soon how this contrasts with coffee drinking in many Mediterranean cultures.

→ I (Still) Want It My Way

Starbucks created a new product in 2005, the *Chantico* (drinkable dessert), which was a hot chocolate meant to mimic the thick, drinkable chocolate found in Europe. It flopped. Starbucks pulled it off the market a year later. Why? Most likely because it could not be customized and adapted to individual tastes.[18]

If you need more convincing that variety and options are valued, look no further than a Starbucks ad that boasted they offer 87,000 combinations of drinks![19]

→ Coffee To-Go

I went to the Starbucks website and saw photos of six different coffees they were promoting; only one was in a mug, made to drink while sitting in the café. One of them had whipped cream on it. I could not see what the others had in them, because they were in the to-go cups, and there was a to-go bag. The point is that almost all the coffee was meant to be drunk on the go.

You can even order your personalized coffee on an app; then when you get to the store and walk in, they smile and say, "Here's your coffee, Rich. Have a great day!"

How great is that? Many people in the US think it's great because it underscores our values of variety, convenience, and customization.

---

18   Elaine Thompson, "In Rare Flop, Starbucks, Scraps Chocolate Drink," NBC News, February 10, 2006, https://www.nbcnews.com/id/wbna11274445.

19   Carl Bialik, "Starbucks Stays Mum on Drink Math," *The Wall Street Journal*, April 2, 2008, https://www.wsj.com/articles/BL-NB-309.

→ Iced Coffee

How many iced-coffee drink varieties could there possibly be? On Starbucks' cold-drinks page (as of the time of this writing), I counted almost sixty options of **cold coffees**, and that doesn't count the Frappuccinos, iced teas, or other cold drinks—or all of the possible personalizations of the drinks you can make.

Compare that to my experience of ordering a *café con hielo* (iced coffee) in Spain. Here it is.

This is literally coffee (a shot of espresso) in one glass, and one cube of ice in another.

To make it work, you then have to strategically pour the coffee into the glass with the ice cube, with such precision and timing, that:

1. You don't spill any of the coffee.

2. You do it quickly enough so that the ice cube doesn't melt and leave you with coffee that's too watered down.

3. You make sure the bar hasn't made a mistake and given you a glass—with ice—that is *smaller* than the amount of liquid you are about to pour in! This has absolutely happened to me before, resulting in a messy overflow situation.

What do these sixty-plus options of cold coffees at Starbucks tell us about a culture? Once again, they are playing to the values of the choice, options, and variety, in order to let us personalize and have things exactly how we want them.

COFFEE DRINKING IN SPAIN AND ITALY: ICEBERGED

Let's compare all of that to coffee drinking in Spain and Italy.

Above the water: people in these Mediterranean cultures rarely get coffee to go. Even up to about ten years ago, if I tried to order a coffee to go, I would either get rejected, because they didn't do coffee to go, or they would put the coffee in a thin *plastic* cup, which would practically start melting in my hand.

Now, that's changed, in recent years, with more tourists coming in—and especially after COVID-19 forced cafés to only offer coffee to go for a time.

However, when you go to a café in Spain or Italy, you mainly see people sitting and drinking their coffee there, usually with others, and you rarely see people sitting alone working on their computers.

The coffee you buy in these Mediterranean cultures is usually pure coffee—without cremes, flavorings, and toppings—so the choices are much more limited.

The size of the coffees is much smaller than in the US. Even the biggest coffee is still smaller than the small size in the US.

If we dive below the water, we see the values and beliefs:

- It's good to take a little break from the go-go-go. It's good to take your time for coffee.

- Having a coffee is a great time to socialize. These are relationship-based cultures vs. the task-based culture of the US, so building relationships around this break (like long lunches together) is important.

- The quality of the coffee is more important than the quantity and more important than being able to add a plethora of flavors.

What about cultures that don't drink so much coffee? Can we still learn about them through their drinking habits?

TEA DRINKING IN BRITAIN

Moving over to the UK, let's talk about British people and tea drinking. I was definitely not a tea drinker when I met my English wife, but when I went back to England, to meet her family and friends, I realized that I had better figure out this whole tea thing, or I was going to get myself into trouble.

As soon as I walked through anyone's door and we said our hellos, the first question out of their mouths was, "Cuppa tea?" This happened at her mom's house, her brother's house, her auntie's house, and every friend's house we went to. I am not exaggerating.

When I said, "No, thank you," to the first offer, I thought she might dump me right there. I definitely wasn't fitting in. I was faced with a look of confusion and, possibly, hurt feelings. So at the next house, I learned my lesson and responded, "Yes, please," but then I came across the next hurdle: "How do you take it?" "Um, milk and sugar, please." The spoonful of sugar was to help this horrible-tasting medicine go down. I didn't like tea, but I was going to prove that I could get through this cultural hurdle.

What I realized about British culture, through tea, is that a cup of tea can solve any problem. You had a bad day? Let's have a cup of tea. Your boyfriend or girlfriend broke up with you? Oh, a nice cuppa tea will sort it out.

According to the UK Tea and Infusions Association (by the way, I love that this association exists), the British consume **100 million cups per day—almost 36 billion cups per year**.[20] That's more than 900 cups a year for every man, woman, and child in Great Britain. In a small sample size of my own, my friends who were back in Wales and Ireland, for three weeks, had four cups a day, as did their families. The English parents of a friend of mine regularly have ten to twelve cups a day.

→ One for Me and One for You

Tea in Britain is a social thing. If you're working in an office and you want a cup of tea, the done thing is to offer to make one for each of your coworkers as well!

Being the cultural chameleon that I claim to be, now whenever my mother-in-law, father-in-law, or my wife's friends from Britain come to visit, the first thing I do is offer them a cup of tea. A hilarious aspect of British culture is how they always seem so pleasantly surprised when you offer it to them—"Oh, that would be lovely, thank you."—as if it wasn't the first thing on their minds already!

So, why is tea such an important part of their culture? Obviously, the history of the United Kingdom cannot be understood without understanding the tea trade and its enormous effect on the economy—historically and currently. We are not going to go into detail, but I highly recommend that if you are going to study or intern in the UK that you figure this out, and soon!

Of course, it's not just Britain, so if you are studying in Turkey, Argentina, China, Ireland, India, and several more countries, I suggest you learn more about the tea-drinking culture, because it will help you understand the people and help you adapt.

By the way, I can say that I actually *enjoy* and look forward to a nice cup of tea these days!

---

20 "FAQs about tea," UK Tea & Infusions Association, accessed February 6, 2022, www.tea.co.uk/tea-faqs.

→ ACT: Hot-Drink Activity

Wherever you are studying, your mission is to find out what the important hot drink is there and why it is important to the culture. Some questions you could ask:

- What's the most important hot drink here?

- Why is it important?

- Do people tend to drink it alone or in a social environment?

- How often or how many cups do people tend to drink?

- Do people typically add anything to the drink?

As you interview people, you will undoubtedly have more questions to ask. If they are appropriate, do it! You'll gain so much knowledge, and who knows, you may just gain a friend—or valuable information to help you get along with a future spouse!

ALCOHOL CULTURE

Now on to a topic that is a favorite of college students in the US: alcohol. When I do talks for US college students on food and culture, and I just flash the word "alcohol" up on the screen, I can see their faces light up; little smirks form, and they get excited to talk about this topic, which is taboo, provocative, and a little naughty.

What is it about alcohol that makes this such a divisive topic, and going back to the story at the beginning of this chapter, what would make it "okay" for people in one culture to drink alcohol at 10:00 a.m., while another culture shuns alcohol at a family diner?

The Atlantic magazine ran an article about Southern Europe's healthy drinking culture.

> Despite widespread consumption of alcohol, Italy has some of the lowest rates of alcoholism in the world. Its residents drink mostly wine and beer, and almost exclusively over meals with other people. When liquor is consumed, it's usually in small quantities, either right before or after a meal. Alcohol is seen as a food, not a drug. Drinking to get drunk is discouraged, as is drinking alone. It is… about as far as you can get from the way many people drink in the United States.[21]

→ ACT: US College-Drinking Culture Iceberged

Imagine a student from outside of the US trying to comprehend the drinking culture of some US college students. What would she see? What behaviors could she observe above the water? Write down your answers before reading mine below.

Above the water:

- It is illegal to drink alcohol if you're under twenty-one years old.

- Even forty-something-year-olds who look nowhere close to twenty-one still get carded (I know from experience).

- Only places with specific, difficult-to-get liquor licenses can serve alcohol.

- Even though it's illegal, many, many college students still drink alcohol.

---

21 Kate Julian, "America Has a Drinking Problem," *The Atlantic,* July/August 2021, www.theatlantic.com/magazine/archive/2021/07/america-drinking-alone-problem/619017/.

- Alcohol is not usually drunk for the nice flavor, to accompany a meal; it's often a means to an end, a way to get drunk.

- Alcohol can be used as a game: beer pong, drinking competitions.

- Most bars have endless beer options to choose from.

- After a night of getting drunk, it's often bragged about.

- Beer can't be served on a Sunday in some places.

- People can be fired from their job if they drink alcohol during the workday.

- Happy hours exist where people can get cheaper alcohol during a limited period of time.

- Some grocery stores only serve 3.2 beer.

BEER PURGATORY

This last one was a big culture shock for me when I moved to Ft. Collins, Colorado, for three months and, during our first stop to stock up the house, I grabbed a twelve-pack of beer. The woman at the register said, "You realize that this is 3.2 beer, right?" I said I didn't, and that I didn't even know what that meant. She explained that grocery stores could only sell beer with less than the normal alcohol level, because of the law there. I thought, *So this is neither a "normal" beer nor a non-alcoholic beer; it's somewhere, caught in the middle, in beer purgatory.* When I asked where I could get a "normal" beer (fully aware of the cultural implications of that word, "normal"), to my pleasant surprise, there was a liquor store right next door where I could get it. So I just needed to walk out the door, walk ten feet, and I could buy beer with the full alcohol content? Fascinating cultural experience.

Let's dive deep into the cultural water, to the bottom of the iceberg, and look at the values, beliefs, and perceptions behind these behaviors to understand them better.

From these behaviors, we can glean that US college students value and believe:

- Competition. We see this through the drinking games and who can drink the most.

- It's okay to break the law in this situation.

- Alcohol can be the social lubricant to make parties less awkward, especially when you don't know anyone.

- It's cool and acceptable to have gotten so drunk that you don't remember what happened the night before.

- There is still a religious aspect to our alcohol consumption, which prohibits alcohol sales in certain locations, and at certain times, because of religious history and tradition.

- You want to get the most for your money. As one student put it, "When I paid €12 ($14) for bottomless margaritas, I wanted to get my money's worth. They're bottomless right?!"

- Alcohol must have a separate place and time, or else it's a problem. When I was at work, I couldn't have a sip of alcohol during the day, for fear of getting severely reprimanded or fired, but then 5:00 p.m. came around, and we'd all leave work and head straight to happy hour to drink, because now "work was done, and we could play." Why did we do that? Why does alcohol hold a separate position and have to be enjoyed that way?"

- I even hear some students say how they rarely, if ever, drink between Sunday and midday Thursday in the US. They wouldn't do that; who does that? But then, from Thursday night through Saturday, they binge drink, get wasted, and get fuzzy on the details of what happened that night, because that's "ok."

Understanding all of this has implications for any college student studying abroad. Like most of what we've seen in this book, the rules that guide alcohol consumption in the US do not usually match the rules for alcohol consumption overseas.

Because alcohol is a powerful drug that alters how we react and affects our decision-making abilities, it's incredibly important for your safety to understand these cultural differences.

And not just for the danger of getting it wrong, but on the positive side, drinking together with the local community is a great way of building trust and relationships when done the right way.

→ ACT: Drinking Alcohol the "Right Way"

What did you learn from your interview(s) with the locals about their views on alcohol where you are studying? Write down how you see the rules of alcohol are the same, or different, from what you are used to and what that means for your time abroad.

→ McDonald's Serves Alcohol

You might not know this if you've never traveled outside of the US, because it does NOT serve alcohol in the US, but you can enjoy a nice cold beer at a McDonald's in France, Belgium, Spain, Greece, The Czech Republic, Italy, and South Korea.

When I was in Russia, what stuck out to me was that McDonald's didn't just serve beer, but it sold vodka—in those little plastic cups with the tinfoil lid that US McDonald's serves orange juice in!

→ Spain's Alcohol Culture: Iceberged

Let's iceberg Spanish alcohol-drinking culture as an example to help you iceberg the alcohol culture of the country you are studying in.

ABOVE THE WATER: EXPLICIT

- Every Spanish café serves alcohol all day (note: I am not including American chains here like Starbucks). The typical image of a bar in Spain would be of all of the alcohol lined up, on a shelf behind the counter, with the coffee machine next to it.

- Morning, noon, and night, you can see people drinking alcohol in restaurants or cafés.

- Most people eat food, while drinking alcohol, and drink in smaller portions.

- The age to legally purchase alcohol is eighteen,[22] but by some accounts, the average age of a first drink is sixteen years old and seven months.[23]

- The *botellón* is a Spanish practice of drinking homemade mixes of alcohol and soda, usually out of plastic bottles, out in public parks or plazas. Mostly teenagers and young adults take part.

BELOW THE WATER: IMPLICIT

From these observations above the water, we can get some of the values and beliefs deep down:

- **Relaxed rules.** When I first got to Barcelona to work, I came with my American lens, and so I purposely did NOT drink any alcohol at a Monday–Friday midday lunch with my colleagues, to prove I was "being good," even though they had no qualms ordering a small beer or wine with lunch. However, I was playing by the US rules, and I soon realized that, if I wanted a glass of wine or beer at lunch, *no pasa nada* (it was absolutely fine), and nobody would think I was doing anything wrong; in fact, they wouldn't think anything about

---

22 "Drinking Age by Country 2022," World Population Review, accessed February 6, 2022, worldpopulationreview. com/country-rankings/drinking-age-by-country.

23 "Informe 2021: Alcohol, Tabaco y Drogas Ilegales en España," Gobierno de España, Sanidad, accessed February 6, 2022, https://pnsd.sanidad.gob.es/profesionales/sistemasInformacion/informesEstadisticas/ pdf/2021OEDA-INFORME.pdf.

it at all. It's not a sign of alcoholism, and it's not typically frowned upon, even during the workweek. As we saw with Italy, levels of alcoholism in Spain are low compared to the rest of the world.

- **Relaxed rules part II.** The legal drinking age is eighteen, but it's common for parents to let their children have sips or small glasses of wine or beer—even at the age of thirteen, fourteen, fifteen—and they don't make a big deal out of it.

- **The importance of being social and relationship building.** Spain is more of a *relationship-based* society compared to the US *task-based* society. Going out and having a drink with tapas to maintain strong relationships—without getting drunk—is an important step towards building trust with colleagues.

- **Views of being drunk.** Once you hit about nineteen or twenty, in Spain, it's not cool to be seen as drunk. In fact, it's very uncool to drink so much that you look and act drunk.

That concludes the sections about food, drink, and culture, but there is MUCH more we could have said. I hope you go out and experience all of the food and culture of where you are studying and where you travel to, as a way to integrate, try new things, and get new perspectives on something that we've all been doing, every day, since the day we were born.

If you are going to drink, please do it responsibly, no matter where you are or how the culture drinks alcohol.

DIVE DEEPER INTO...
→ Drinks and their effect on the world today:
Tom Standage, *A History of the World in 6 Glasses* (New York: Walker & Co., 2005).

→ American drinking culture vs. Europe's drinking culture:
Kate Julian, "America Has a Drinking Problem," *The Atlantic,* July/August, 2021, https://www.theatlantic.com/magazine/archive/2021/07/america-drinking-alone-problem/619017/.

Chapter 13

WELL-BEING ABROAD

CARING FOR YOUR BODY AND MIND

Study abroad is seeing an increase in the number of students dropping out, before they even arrive, or getting on site and leaving, after the first few days, because they can't handle the changes they are experiencing. Students feel less prepared, more anxious, and more overwhelmed than I've seen in over twenty-five years working in this field.

Remember, from the intro to this book, that even I was ready to pack it all in, quit my new dream job, and move back to the comforts of home, after four months, because I wasn't sure what I had gotten myself into and why I did this to myself.

The good news is that I made it through; so do hundreds of thousands of students per year, and so can you.

Study abroad can be stressful; this chapter helps you learn tips and strategies to maintain a healthy body and healthy mind, so you can get the most out of this amazing opportunity.

ARE YOU EXHAUSTED YET? THIS IS NORMAL

Living abroad is physically exhausting because we are no longer on cultural autopilot, like we are back home, and everything we do saps more energy from us than we are used to. Every step of the way, and every action of the day, takes more out of us, especially in those first weeks.

If you feel this way, don't worry; it's normal. If you are not feeling that way, that's great too. Some people feel it at different times throughout the experience. Part of the solution to not having it drag you down is simply knowing that it could happen.

→ Why Do Students Tend to Get Sick More Often During the First Weeks of Study Abroad?

Imagine a student called Zoe who is studying for a semester in Copenhagen: she wakes up in a homestay and has to speak Danish as soon as she's awake; figure out how to turn on a new shower; think about whether she is allowed to just take some breakfast or has to ask for it, and if she has to ask for it, how she does that. What are the vocab words if she needs to say please and thank you? At first, getting to school means figuring out a new public-transportation system or a walk through unfamiliar streets—putting her fight-or-flight response on high alert—and she's unsure how long it will take. She gets to school and is not sure where to go; she doesn't understand the signs, and the school she is at is not as detail-oriented as what she's used to. And that's just the logistics. Maybe she hasn't dressed appropriately or brought the right materials; she doesn't seem to fit in and, worse, feels like she stands out and everyone is staring. She's made it through class time but then has four hours of free time and is unsure what to do. Back home, on campus, she never has free time, because every last minute is booked up in her agenda with class, clubs, sports, study groups, work, etc.

The percentage of students getting sick in the first weeks is much higher, because their bodies and minds have to navigate everything that is new—which is a lot—and their bodies don't have as much strength to fight off viruses.

Don't let this scare you off! Remember, the goal of this book is to prepare you for these experiences and make days like these disappear, quickly, so you can start making the most of your time abroad. Soon enough, Zoe is going to amaze herself at how she can speak to the host mom as soon as she wakes up; doesn't think twice about how to get to school; and goes straight over to her group of local friends, to chat about the weekend. And instead of being a stressor, the four hours of free time bring her joy, for all that she can experience in that time.

However, there will be days and moments of stress, without question. That's what happens when you go abroad, and as we've said, those are some of the greatest opportunities for growth and learning; but that doesn't make it any easier while you're in the thick of it.

→ ACT: How Do You Deal with Stress Now?

To prepare yourself, think about how you deal with stress now. What are your go-to methods? What helps you feel less stressed? It's important to know that, now, so when you are abroad and go through the stressors, you are ready with a plan.

Write down all of the ways you deal with stress back home.

Which of those things will you be able to continue doing while abroad?

If there is something you can't do, what could you replace it with?

Here's the good news: dealing with all of this stress abroad; understanding yourself and how you deal with it; and coming up with a plan to overcome it won't just help you while you're abroad. It will serve you throughout life. When you learn more about what causes you stress or discomfort, you're also better able to predict it and prevent it. When you learn what's behind the anxiety, you're better prepared.

In fact, it's even a *professional* growth lesson. A common interview question is: *Tell me about a time you were stressed? What did you do to overcome it?* It's at that point, in the interview for your dream job, that you smile, relax, and nail the answer.

MAINTAINING A HEALTHY BODY

→ Sleep

Getting a good amount of sleep is incredibly important, especially when you first get to the new country. The students we see who get sick right away are the ones who are not getting enough sleep. I know it's tempting; you want to jump right into it, go out, stay up late, etc., but there will be time for that. When you first arrive, and your body and mind are making all of these adjustments, getting sleep is one of the best things you can do.

→ Exercise

Getting exercise has not only been proven to keep people healthier but also to keep them happier. People who suffer from depression are told— almost mandated—to get endorphins pumping through their bodies with exercise. I can't stress this enough: make sure you get plenty of physical exercise when you are abroad. How can you do this?

- **Gym:** By joining a gym, you get a two-for-one deal; you get to stay fit and exercise while also giving yourself loads of opportunities for cultural observation and a chance to meet locals.

- **Outdoor Exercise:** Maybe a gym is not for you, or you don't want to spend the money. No problem; walk or jog around the city. Find different safe areas that you can explore. Join a running group so you can meet new people.

- **Hiking:** Walking through forests or mountains is both good for your body and good for your soul.

- **Cycling:** Rent a bike and explore while getting exercise.

- **Groups:** Join some kind of activity that you like. If you are interested in yoga or Pilates, find a place that does that. Do you like dancing? Take a dance class. It would be especially cool if you could take a dance class to learn the typical dance(s) of the country that you are in.

Find something that motivates you to exercise and stick to it. It is one of the best ways to beat stress and, possibly, get more immersed in the culture.

HEALTHY MIND

Remember—way back to the introduction of this book—my warning about social media—STUDY ABROAD IS NOT YOUR FRIENDS' SOCIAL-MEDIA POSTS. Someone may try to make you believe that what you see on their Instagram or TikTok was their whole experience, but they are photoshopping the truth and only showing you the highlights. There are definitely low points as well, but if your expectations come from their highlight reel, then when you have those low points yourself, you might start thinking, *What is wrong with me?!* Nothing is wrong with you. It is normal. The only wrong thing is trying to get a picture of what a study abroad experience is like by following others' social media.

I say this because it can have a big effect on your well-being to make these comparisons between your real experience and someone else's virtual highlight reel.

➜» FAST TRACK ACT: KEEP A GRATITUDE JOURNAL

It's very easy to get caught up in the negative when you are out of your comfort zone and going through new challenges all the time. In fact, our brains are wired to find the negative around us, because that has helped keep us alive and avoid danger.

This means that we need to make an extra effort to see the positive, but luckily, we can train our brains to do that.

Let's take a lesson from the fields of Positive Psychology and Cognitive Behavioral Therapy. They both suggest the enormous benefits of keeping a **journal** of the **positive aspects** of life. My suggestion is that you keep a journal where you write down all of the positive aspects of your life abroad and the **new culture** you are in. Try to get in the habit of doing this **every day**.

The gratitude journal is simple: every day, you write down three things that you are grateful for that day. It could be someone who did something for you, something you accomplished, something that made you happy, or something small like the smell of a freshly made crepe in France.

The great thing about doing this activity is that you are training yourself to feel this gratitude, and you find yourself noticing it more and more, which can send the same endorphins through your body that exercise does.

Try it for two weeks, maybe every night before you go to bed. If it's not for you and you stop, that's okay, but maybe you'll love it and can keep it going for the rest of your experience, and even once you get home.

NOTICE THE NEGATIVE, BUT DON'T FOCUS ON IT

Don't worry if you find yourself thinking of the negative too. That's fine! You should also write down some of those "negative" things because you'll be amazed and entertained, when you read back on them later, and realize that maybe they weren't as negative as you thought.

In fact, if you didn't see anything negative, I would be concerned that you are not doing enough to get out of your comfort zone and not pushing yourself to engage in the new culture.

And don't worry if it's really hard to see the positive during certain periods abroad. It is completely normal and happens to almost everyone. Give yourself a break, and some extra time, if that is the case.

I know a student who kept a journal but was caught in a negative loop, **only** focusing on the "negative" aspects of the culture: stores being closed on Sundays; the extremely slow pace of life; people invading his personal space; not having his friends around; missing out on things back home; and eagerly counting down the days until **he finally could leave**.

Then he turned his mindset around by seeing Sundays as a time to read more and take up a new hobby, slowing down his usual frantic pace of life, spending more time with new acquaintances instead of with technology, and eventually, sadly, counting down the days until **he HAD to go home**.

Of course, that person was me, and I'm still abroad, twenty years later! I look back on that journal now, and I feel such confidence. I feel like if I could go through that difficult time in my life, now I can do anything. I'm glad that I was able to shift that mindset!

These are tools that I firmly believe in, but of course, they do not replace professional psychological help if that's what is needed. If you are feeling especially down, withdrawn, anxious, depressed, or worse, and you feel like it's beyond the typical ups and downs of study abroad, go get professional help. Get advice from your program, or the university where you are studying, to find out who you can speak with. More and more of our students find that seeing a psychologist or therapist, in the city where they are studying, or keeping in touch with their professional help from back home, through regular video calls, helps tremendously.

STAY IN TOUCH...BUT NOT TOO MUCH

When I studied abroad, I spoke on the phone with my mom, once a week, on Sundays. In between, we would write letters. Handwritten letters! Now, the concept seems incredible—that you would write out what you are doing and feeling in a letter—but it takes a week for it to get to them, and by then you've done so many other new and exciting things and might be feeling very differently.

There are some great reasons to write these letters:

- You will have them as memories, almost like a journal, for years and years. Not like a tweet or a Snapchat.

- They are a nice, slow way of reflecting on the experience. Your thought process is different when you handwrite something instead of typing it on electronics.

- You will make the day of whoever receives them! When was the last time you received anything handwritten? It's probably been a while, but I'm sure it was something special.

→ ACT: Write a Handwritten Letter to Someone Back Home

Grab yourself a favorite pen and some nice paper and find yourself a cozy spot—it might be a comfortable place where you're staying, or out in a café, or a park, or on a hill with inspirational views—and write at least a one-page letter to someone back home. Don't tell the person that it's coming, and you'll see how surprised they are when they get it, because they probably haven't received anything like this in...ever.

DISCONNECT

Students are constantly connected with their friends and family back home, through texts, emails, phone calls, video calls, or through what I call "unconscious communication," like social media channels that are sent from one person to many. The problem with being constantly connected back home is that it's harder to be in the moment abroad, and you miss out on so much.

How do you become more independent and gain confidence if you are dependent on someone back home to help you out?

How do you become more resilient, when things get tough, while relying on support from a parent vs. trying to do it yourself?

How do you explore when you always use Google Maps to get you around?

How do you engage with locals if you are always head down on your phone?

When I asked a student, at the end of his summer internship, what he was most proud of, his answer wasn't about something he'd accomplished in his internship; in fact, it had nothing to do with the workplace. He traveled to another country, on the weekend, by himself, and his hotel wasn't in the city center as he'd thought when he booked it. He didn't realize it, though, until the bus dropped him off. Then he realized that he had no cell coverage because he was in another country, and he would have to figure this out on his own. He went to the tourist information office where he got a paper map, and they sent him in the right direction. Then he had to ask people, along the way, with his limited language skills. It took him an hour, but he got there, and he felt great that he had done it—even better than if it had all been easy. That was his biggest accomplishment of the entire summer.

After that, he never felt stressed or worried, when he was lost or things didn't go as planned, which is a great life lesson—not to mention a powerful anecdote for a job interview.

→ ACT: Tell Mom and Dad You'll Talk to Them in a Week

Sometimes you are perfectly happy to stay disconnected, but it's your parents who are writing to you all the time and checking in. That is understandable. I'm a parent, and I know what it's like. Try to tell your parents that you want to disconnect for several days. If you can't think of the words, try this script next time you are on the phone:

> Mom, Dad, I'm having such a great experience. I'm doing amazing things, meeting wonderful people, and even feeling okay out of my comfort zone. Here's my next comfort-zone challenge for myself—"disconnect" from people back home for one week. I want to be more present here, but when I am constantly on my phone or computer with people back home, I can't do that. It might be tough, for all of us, but let's try it. I'll call you in a week. Thanks again for helping me have this awesome experience!

→ ACT: Stay in Touch with Others Who Are Abroad

If you have friends studying in other countries, they are great people to stay in touch with. They might be going through their own ups and downs and would love to hear from you.

My suggestion is to get on a phone or video call with them, once in a while; don't just be in touch with texting or short bursts of written communication on social media. Ask them how they are doing, what cultural differences they've noticed, what has been the best part of their experience, and what has been the most challenging. Those answers—rather than the illusion created by their Snapchat stories, Instagram photos, or TikTok videos—should give you true insight into their experience.

→ ACT: Spend Time on Your Own

Study abroad is the perfect time to get some "me time." If you are like the thousands of students I've worked with, your home life is constantly busy—there is rarely a free moment. Take advantage of the time abroad to spend time on your own doing…whatever you want to do. Maybe for the first time in a long time, you have no one else to worry about, no activities to run to, and nowhere to be, so now is the time to take advantage of that.

Spend some of that time on your own, without electronic stimuli—that is, no music, no podcast, no headphones at all. Write down how it felt to do that. Was it difficult? Was it refreshing? If this is not something you normally do, back home, do you want to find more time to do it now?

TAKE CARE

It bears repeating that your whole time abroad will not be a highlight reel; there will be tough times, and those times could affect your well-being. Make sure you are prepared for this, and then take steps to keep a healthy body and a healthy mind so you can make the most of your time.

Getting through those tough times was hard for me, but looking back, I am so glad that I went through them so I could come out the other side feeling stronger than ever.

And remember, if things are especially tough and you feel like you should seek professional help, then don't hesitate to do so.

DIVE DEEPER INTO...

→ Creating memorable experiences:

Chip Heath and Dan Heath, *The Power of Moments: Why Certain Experiences Have Extraordinary Impact* (Delran: Simon & Schuster, 2017).

→ Creating better habits:

James Clear, *Atomic Habits: An Easy & Proven Way to Build Good Habits & Bread Bad Ones*, (Garden City: Avery, 2018).

Chapter 14

DON'T STAND SO CLOSE TO ME

PERSONAL SPACE

I wanted to go all out on my fortieth birthday, so I rented a bar and invited about fifty friends—locals from Barcelona, Americans, Brits, and several other nationalities—to my dress-up party. The theme of the party was: the USA. They had to come dressed like an American—however they interpreted that idea.

There were Al Capone-style gangsters, cheerleaders, Marilyn Monroe, Michael Jackson, a cowboy with an inflatable horse between his legs, and a 1950s waitress who spent the entire night on roller skates; and then there was the couple from Barcelona who came with a giant Hula-Hoop orbiting around their bodies, held up by suspenders, and a sign on their chests that read: "Caution: you're trespassing my personal space."

The difference in how cultures perceive personal space may be one of the most visceral—that is, deep and instinctual—and cringe-inducing differences when you are thrown into new cultural waters. Without ever having seen it written down, we have an ingrained sense of what feels right and wrong to us when it comes to personal space—and it permeates so much of how we act and what we do, every day.

To make the most out of your connections with people across cultures, you must understand personal space.

GREETINGS ACROSS CULTURES

→ ACT: Greetings: Yours and Theirs

Step 1: Write down the answers to these questions: How do you greet your best friend? Your parents? Someone you've just met for the first time? Your teachers? How much physical contact do you have with them, or how much distance do you keep between you? Does it change with how well you know the person?

Step 2: Now, write down how you've observed people greeting each other in your host country. What type of distance is between them?

Step 3: Have you had to greet anyone in the new country differently than you are used to back home? How did it make you feel? Have you gotten used to it yet, or does it feel awkward?

Step 4: Iceberg the greetings in your host culture. What lies beneath the water? What values and beliefs would you say lead to your host culture greeting the way it does?

→ The Handshake and Wave Greeting in the US

In the US, we often greet people by shaking hands with them. In a business scenario, the proper thing to do is to shake hands; but we even do it in a social situation when we are meeting a friend of a friend for the first time.

Or with a bigger group, it's absolutely fine to wave hello to everyone, at once, without going person to person.

By now, you know what's coming… can we iceberg that?

What do we observe with the handshake or the wave greeting?

- A handshake automatically puts a personal distance of two arms' lengths between you and the other person.

- A wave maintains even more distance.

- In business, it's typical to give a firm handshake.

- No touching with the other hand is necessary with a handshake.

- It's a quick way of greeting many people.

This demonstrates—as we saw by the birthday-party super costume—Americans love to have a large personal space and to keep our distance. Also, as we know, time is money, so we don't want to "waste time" by shaking hands with everyone when a quick hello and wave would do.

We also judge people by their handshake: they are trustworthy if they give a firm handshake but, on the other hand, maybe lack confidence by offering a "limp fish" handshake. Add to that all of the nonverbal communication and messages we talked about in Chapter 10 (eye contact, smiling, etc.), and you've made a judgment about someone within the first couple seconds of meeting them. This has implications for assumptions people will make about you in the new culture.

→ Iceberg Greetings with Kisses

By now, your powers of iceberging should be close to superpowers, so let's compare a US handshake to greetings around the world that use kisses. France, Italy, Columbia, Belgium, Croatia, Argentina, Hungary, and many more have some version of kissing to greet—even people you are meeting for the first time.

Step 1: Above the Water: Observable and Explicit

- People greeting by kissing on the cheek once, twice, three, or more times.

- There is physical contact.

- People do this even when they are meeting the person for the first time.

- Sometimes there is also touching with the other hand: on the shoulder, with a hug, etc.

Step 2: Below the Water: Implicit, Values, and Beliefs

- Close contact between strangers is okay or "normal."

- Keeping a distance when greeting—either with a handshake or just a wave—could be seen as cold.

- There is no need to save time by just waving. In Spain, if you meet up with a group of ten people, for example, you do *"dos besos"* ("two kisses") with everyone, when you arrive and when you leave.

→》 FAST TRACK ACT: MAKING THE UNCOMFORTABLE...LESS UNCOMFORTABLE

One of my favorite activities to do with students is called **The Speed Interview**. Feel free to grab a friend and try it right now. Here's what you do:

1. Find a partner you are going to interview. The questions for that person could be anything at all, but you're only going to have thirty seconds total to get the question and the answer out for both of you. If you are doing it with another student studying abroad, I suggest asking: What are your goals for your time abroad? What do you hope to get out of it by the time you finish? Don't start yet...

2. Now that you have your partner, set a timer for thirty seconds.

3. Now, stand **toe-to-toe** with the other person. That's right; you need to have your toes touching the toes of the other person. Both feet.

4. Start the timer.

5. Go!

The students' answers to the interview questions don't really matter to me. I want to know: how did this make you *feel*?

I say "making the uncomfortable less uncomfortable" rather than fully "comfortable" because...remember when I said personal space issues are visceral? We feel them so deeply that this exercise makes American students squirm. Students who have never done yoga in their lives some-how perform backbends that would make yoga instructors jealous, just to put some distance between them and their partners. Students cross their arms in front of themselves to have some semblance of personal space, eye contact is almost nonexistent, and still, the thirty seconds seems like an eternity.

A little secret—this activity is actually called Toe-to-Toe, but if I say that at the beginning, it gives it all away, so if you get some of your friends to do it, keep the secret until the end.

This will come in handy when you step into any European elevator. Americans coming to Europe get immediate culture shock when they enter a tiny elevator that would, in the US, typically be for one or two people; but here the sign says, "Capacity 4," and they are squeezed in, like sardines, next to strangers!

CULTURAL BLUNDERS: PERSONAL SPACE AND GREETINGS

Understanding personal-space issues could mean the difference between making new friends and ... punching someone in the stomach.

Let me explain. We had a male student who went to the same café several mornings in a row—partially because he liked the *café con leche* and *croissant de chocolate* and partially because he had a crush on the young woman working there. He told me how he was surprised and a little annoyed at the "lack of customer service," because even though he had been there several days in a row, she hadn't really paid him any special attention.

Then, finally, the following week, when he went in (as he tells it), her face lit up, and she gave him a big *buenos días* with a smile, and even came out from the back to greet him. He got so excited and nervous he went to give her the firmest handshake he could, while she was going in for the two kisses. The end result was that, as she leaned in for the *dos besos*, he JABBED her in the stomach with his outstretched hand!

In addition to the importance of learning how to greet properly in different cultures, this is also a good reminder of how, when we are stressed or under pressure, we revert to our instincts, and our cultural autopilot does what feels most normal.

→ ACT: Find Out How to Greet. Observe, Ask, Research, and Participate

The country you are studying in may have a greeting that will be uncomfortable for you at first and take some getting used to, depending on the greeting culture you are coming from. You might be experiencing the German knock on the table, the Moroccan quick, light handshake and then hand to the heart, Thai "praying hands," a Japanese bow, a big bear hug, or something entirely different.

It's now up to you to find out what those rules are. They are often unwritten, so you'll be best off observing or asking, if you can't find them by researching. Be sure to find out the "how" (above the water) but also the "why" (below the water) because understanding why people act the way that they do helps us to adapt.

Once you get used to the new greeting, just remember to switch when you go to another culture. If you go back to the US, with a kissing greeting, you'll have a very Borat-like uncomfortable situation on your hands.

→ "Close" Talkers

Maybe you know someone who is (as comedian Jerry Seinfeld so aptly dubbed the type) a "close talker." This is someone who stands a little too close for comfort when talking to you. Of course, that comfort level partially comes from your national culture but also from you as an individual.

This is one of those unwritten rules: I don't think we are ever told to stand 3.94 feet away from someone we don't know well when we are talking to them. We just know what feels right—and definitely what **doesn't** feel right. We also judge that someone who is "too close" might be pushy or aggressive, and if they stand "too far," they might seem standoffish.

When I do the toe-to-toe Speed Interview activity with students, I follow it up with this: I ask one student to come up to the front of the class and talk to me about what they learned from their partner. That student comes and faces me, as if only talking to me, and if they are American, they will inevitably stand at the typical distance apart, or maybe even a bit further because they don't know me well.

Then comes the fun part. As they are speaking, I slowly start moving closer to them, and I can see they visibly get uncomfortable, usually stop talking, nervously smile, and sometimes clam up completely. When I get to a distance that is not uncommon for some cultures, even I still feel uncomfortable with it, but after so much training in a close-talking culture, I've learned to handle it.

My discomfort was really brought home to me, not long ago, when a Spanish professor walked up to me in the hallway. As he walked up, I said, *"Hola, qué* tal*?!"* ("Hi, how's it going?") He walked up, right in my face, as he's used to, and said, "Oh, awful, I've had this terrible cold, for a week, that I just can't shake." Arrgh! I tried to keep cool, but I slowly inched backward, and he commenced the "personal-space shuffle" towards me, to keep the distance he felt comfortable with, until I backed into a wall and could go no further.

Not five minutes later, I ran into an American professor who was visiting, and I said, "Hey, how's it going?" and reached out to shake his hand. He put his hand up to stop me, backed up, and said, "Rich, don't get close to me; I've got a terrible cold." And we maintained the "I-have-a-cold distance," which I don't think has ever been officially researched but should be.

An important takeaway here is not just learning what the greeting is in the culture you are going to, but how it makes **the other person feel if you don't greet in the same way**.

If you are in a country that does a kiss greeting and you refuse to, because it makes you feel uncomfortable, and just plan to wave or shake hands, what will they think about you? They will think that you're not adaptable, don't know the proper way to fit into the culture, or worse, think that you are cold and distant and purposely putting space between you, meaning maybe you are not trustworthy and not friendly. All of those things could be false, but it's the perception that's most important.

In order to make proper connections with people of other cultures, understanding your own and their comfort levels with personal space is massively important.

PERSONAL SPACE: OTHER ASPECTS OF CULTURE

Cultures with closer personal-space distances than you are used to can lead to other areas of discomfort and confusion as well.

There were times, especially when I first got to Spain, that I got really angry because people were too close to me or actually touching me. Taking the metro to my classes in Madrid was incredibly frustrating at first. We would be coming up to a stop that wasn't mine, on the crowded train, and people would just put their hands on me and literally shove me out of the way. More than once, I responded by turning and glaring at the person, with a threatening stare, ready to defend myself from this "attack" only to find that it was a little old woman who was worried she'd miss her stop!

Now that I understand personal-space differences, I don't get angry when it happens. I understand now that my value of a larger personal space used to mean that, if someone I didn't know touched me, it felt like an invasion (notice the violent undertone of the word "invasion") or a threat. Other cultures don't see it that way at all.

If they give two kisses to a stranger, why can't they also touch a stranger who is in their way when they need to get off the metro?

The problem is mine for not understanding, not adapting, and not moving.

It's easier said than done when we are so used to seeing things one way. In the US, in that same scenario, the proper thing to do is ask, "Excuse me; are you getting off here? Sorry, I just need to get by," and say it with a smile. But here, the rules have changed, and I need to play by the new rules, not the ones I am used to.

→ Waiting in Line

Other examples include **waiting in line**. I notice now, when I go back to the US and wait in line, people leave a good two-person (or more) space between themselves and the person in front of them; but in cultures with smaller personal space, it's perfectly normal for someone to stand right behind the other person, almost touching, even when there is room not to have to do that.

→ No "Excuse Me?"

It also comes into play when **eating meals**. I was always taught that the polite thing to do at a table, when you needed something passed to you, was to say: "Excuse me, could you pass the salt please?" which is why I was so taken aback here, when someone sitting next to me was happy to reach across my body and my plate to grab something that was on the other side, without an "excuse me" or an apology.

But why would they apologize? If that space is not so "personal," then there is no need to apologize. But, in the mind of someone with a bigger personal space, they apologize because they have invaded our area.

I sometimes get myself in trouble, when I go back to the US, because I have adopted some of these new rules and interiorized them, so I do them without thinking. For example, I'll be at the grocery store in the US and walk in between a shopper and whatever they are looking at, without saying "sorry" or "excuse me," and I get dirty looks.

→ Touching

Because of this personal-space difference, touching is more common, in general, in cultures with a smaller personal space. In Spain, waiters will happily put their hands on your shoulder, when answering a question you've asked them, without thinking this is an invasion. If that happened in many places in the US, you'd probably ask to speak to a manager to report some type of harassment.

Of course, this is not true in all parts of the US. I've been to smaller cities and towns, especially in the South, where it is "okay" or "normal" for a server to call you honey or sweetheart and lightly touch your arm while talking.

→ ACT: Personal-Space Differences Where You Are Studying

What differences in personal space have you noticed?

Step 1: Write down all of the examples that you can. How does it make you feel when people act differently than how you would anticipate or what you are used to?

How well do you feel you've adapted to the differences? How well do you understand the why behind those differences and then adapt accordingly?

Step 2: Next time you are with someone from that culture, mention that these things stuck out to you and have a conversation about why.

→ Personal Space: COVID-19

It would be a missed opportunity not to write about the impact of COVID-19 on culture. This could apply to several of the ideas discussed in this book, but the personal-space issue has obviously been greatly affected, because laws are in place to *socially distance* at the time of writing this book. No matter how close people were comfortable with before, for COVID-19 prevention, they are forced, in most scenarios, to be six feet or two meters apart. This also means that the cultures accustomed to greeting with kisses have mostly stopped greeting each other this way. I say "mostly" because I still have some friends—and see some people on the street—giving the two kisses even during a pandemic. Their cultural urge to be close to someone, and viewing a kiss as a proper greeting, is stronger than their fear of catching the virus.

DIVE DEEPER INTO...

→ Proxemics—the study of personal space:

Edward T. Hall, *The Hidden Dimension* (Garden City: Anchor Books. 1969).

→ Greetings across cultures:

Too many to specify here, but YouTube has many videos of different greetings across cultures.

Chapter 15

IT'S ABOUT TIME

TIME IS MONEY. OR IS IT?

Imagine you are twenty years old, and a ninety-year-old billionaire inventor (let's just picture this as Elon Musk in the future) has figured out how two people can switch ages. He offers you all of his money to switch places with him—you become the ninety-year-old billionaire, and he gets to be twenty years old, with your bank account. Would you do it?

I think that almost anyone in the world would say no. Our time on earth—our time to live—is more precious and important than money. So why are we so focused on gathering wealth at the expense of our time, which we can never get back?

Have you ever noticed that we use the same words and phrases to describe time and money?

Waste time, waste money

Invest time, invest money

Spend time, spend money

Save time, save money

Make time, make money

We talk about time and money in the same way in the US because, to many Americans, one of the worst things you can do is waste their time. That slows down productivity, and productivity equals achievement, which equals money and winning at the American dream. As we'll see, this is not a shared value around the world, and therefore, your approach to time affects the connections and relationships you will forge while abroad.

This chapter offers tips and strategies to observe cultural differences related to time, to analyze the why behind those differences, and what it means to cultural adaptation.

~~~~~~

NO APOLOGIES

I met two other Americans and three Catalans for lunch in Barcelona. We had a 1:30 p.m. reservation. I showed up, fifteen minutes early, to sit by the beach and have a drink while I waited for the others. Two of the locals arrived at 1:30 p.m. on the dot, one other local showed up about four minutes after that, and the two Americans arrived at 1:35 p.m. One of the Americans (who has been living in Spain for ten years) came over and said hello to everyone, and the other American woman, who was just visiting from the US, profusely apologized for being late. She was the only one to apologize.

On a recent business Zoom call, an American colleague apologized for coming one minute late.

~~~~~~

Since time is such a valued commodity in the US, if we dare show up a few minutes late to a meeting, we must apologize—even at a social gathering.

When I first got to Spain, I would call friends to apologize for arriving at a dinner meeting five minutes after the organized time, and they would laugh at me and say, "Why did you even call? I am going to be ten minutes late, and I wasn't going to warn you!"

What does all of this mean for cross-cultural adjustment? We have to adjust our time mindsets to be able to adapt. Where you might see a culture as rude for arriving late or canceling at the last minute, they might see you as inflexible and unnecessarily rigid. In my experience, this can be one of the most frustrating things about living in another culture, but, as we said before, knowing why people do what they do helps us to adapt.

DON'T WASTE MY TIME!

These can be little incidents, like when I have a barber's appointment at 9:30 a.m., and I arrive at 9:28 but end up waiting until 9:55, and they call me over with no apology or even an acknowledgment of the tardiness. (P.S. Yes, I am bald, but I went for a beard trim).

Or these can be rather big incidents, like when I used to get annoyed at my colleagues, and even my boss, for wasting too much of my time. When we had a one-on-one meeting at 11:00 a.m., I would show up in my boss's office at 10:58; he'd call me in to sit down, and then I would wait while he finished whatever he was doing. We would start the meeting at 11:03, :04, :05. No apologies.

When we would have team meetings—and there were only four of us—the meeting would start even later because the others would show up "late" while I was the only fool who had gotten there before the hour to be prepared when the clock said that I was supposed to be there.

When I noted the observation to my boss that "it's interesting that, in the US, people show up on time for meetings, and here it's okay to show up late," he said that line that is emblazoned in my brain: "Rich, you have to adapt to the culture; the culture will not adapt to you. If you can't do that, you are going to have problems here." Ouch. That was a powerful culture punch to the gut.

But he was absolutely right. I had not yet internalized that what seems rude to one person can definitely be seen as normal to another. I had to adapt.

And I did. I still found it hard to arrive "late" to these meetings, but if a meeting started at noon, I would arrive at noon (I would still be the first one there), and I would bring work with me, so as not to "waste my time." I now realize something even deeper, that if I had just taken those few minutes before meetings to relax and clear my mind, that would have been just as useful to my productivity, but I felt like I had to be busy doing something.

→ ACT: Two Steps, Five Whys—Iceberging Punctuality

Why would Americans apologize when arriving late? Let's iceberg that, using a trick called the Five Whys. The Five Whys is a great activity to help us dive deeper and deeper under the water, to discover more values and beliefs that drive behavior.

Step 1: Above the water, we observe that Americans tend to apologize for not arriving "on time." **Why?**

Step 2: Below the water.

Because there is a value and a belief, in much of the US, that if you are not early, you are late. **Why?**

Because time is such a precious commodity for Americans that we don't want to waste it by waiting around. **Why** is it a precious commodity?

Because we could be using that time to be productive? **Why** is that important?

Because productivity is a sign of hard work, and that is a value? **Why?**

Because that is one way of proving worth, achievement, and success.

→ ACT: Reflection on Punctuality

When you are back in the US, do you tend to be punctual?

What do you do when you're late? Do you apologize? Why?

What does punctuality mean where you are studying? What does it mean to be "on time"? Do people apologize when they arrive late? How have you adapted to that?

BE AWARE OF YOUR PUNCTUALITY

I was giving a "Working Across Cultures: Intercultural Differences in International Business" talk to a group of students at a university in Barcelona, and I asked them: "If your class starts at 10:00 a.m., what time are you in your seats, ready for class?" The answer was a collective giggle and then a consensus of two to three minutes after the hour. When I asked if the teacher gets upset, there was a bigger laugh—also by the teacher—who said he usually doesn't get there until five minutes after, then starts setting up! Does anyone get upset about it? No! This goes back to the idea that there is no absolute right or wrong in this case, but it's got to be right for that context.

If a Spanish student goes to a US university and arrives at every class two to three minutes late—because *no pasa nada* (no big deal); it's just a few minutes; everyone does it in Spain—that's not going to fly.

This is not to say that, when you are studying abroad, you should automatically arrive late everywhere if that's what the culture does. Definitely not! It's best to observe the difference in punctuality and then adapt to it as necessary, because it will not adapt to you.

I am now so used to the laid-back—from my lens—Spanish way of time that I need to be careful with business appointments, or even social appointments, in the US, because my instinct would allow me to arrive after the scheduled time. However, I fight that urge, knowing that I would upset people and be considered rude.

SCHEDULING AND PERCEPTIONS OF TIME

→ ACT: Your Daily Schedule

Write down your typical daily schedule on an average Monday through Friday when you are back at home at school. Include waking-up times, meal times, class times, meetings, studying times, bedtime, etc. Compare that to your schedule abroad. What's changed and why? How do you feel about those changes?

→》 FAST TRACK ACT: INTERVIEW A LOCAL

I'll give you an excuse to ask people about their views of time; here's a fun little assignment. Find some locals to talk to and ask them these questions:

- What time do you typically eat breakfast, lunch, dinner, or any other meals throughout the day? How long does each of those meals last?

- If you are meeting a friend out at a restaurant, for a meal at a certain time, what time do you show up?

- If a friend has invited you to their place for a meal at a certain time, what time do you show up?

- If you have a meeting for work at a certain time, what time do you show up? What about colleagues?

- If you have a study-group session with other students at a certain time, what time do you show up? What about the others?

- Do you apologize if you show up after the time you had arranged?

- How do you feel if others show up after the time you had arranged?

- Why do you think you have the sense of time that you do?

- Do you belong to a gym? If so, what time do you usually go? When is the gym most crowded?

- What time do you tend to wake up during the week? On the weekends?

- How much sleep do you tend to get per night?

Now compare your schedule to a local's schedule. Where are the similarities, and where are the differences?

My entire perception of time and schedules has shifted by living abroad. Take this example: when my wife got a job at a large Spanish company, her working hours were 9:00 a.m.–1:40 p.m. and then 3:00 p.m.–6:30 p.m., so she had an obligatory hour and twenty-minute lunch break built in and then finished work at 6:30 p.m. To her English mind, and my American mind, finishing work at 6:30 p.m. was quite late in the day, but when she told our Spanish friend about the job and the schedule, she replied: "Wow, that's great. You finish work early and still have the whole afternoon ahead of you."

It's just a matter of perspective—for our friend, getting off at 6:30 p.m. was early. Seeing that most stores in Barcelona stay open until 9:00 p.m. and dinner doesn't start until 9:00 p.m., that made sense! In my American mind, the day has already started to wind down at 6:00 p.m.

This view of time and daily schedules pervades everything we do, including eating times, sleeping times, and working times, and not just the schedules, but the duration as well.

→ ACT: Eat When the Locals Eat

As we saw, in the food chapter, eating schedules can vary greatly from culture to culture.

This isn't so much an activity as just a general suggestion to get more out of your time abroad: eat when the locals eat! Try not to cling to your schedules from home. This will break you out of your comfort zone and be a good exercise to flex your cultural-adjustment muscles.

HOW MUCH CAN WE CONTROL TIME?

→ ACT: How Structured Are Your Days/Weeks/Months?

Review your schedule back home, which you wrote down at the beginning of this chapter. Are you scheduling activities one after another? Do your calendar and daily agenda rule your life? Is your week fully planned out and your month too?

If so, you are showing that you view time as something that can be controlled, and you are assuming, based on your knowledge of yourself and your own culture, that things will "run like clockwork." When you plan to meet with someone, at a certain time, you expect them to turn up, and you expect it to last however long you have predetermined it will last. How does it make you feel if someone cancels last-minute?

I would guess that you have your days and weeks tightly scheduled if you are from the US. We tend to do that because of the value of punctuality we mentioned before, and when someone says they will be there at x time, they will be there at x time.

→ Shop Opens at 9:00 a.m....ish

That's not the same everywhere. It was 1:00 p.m., and I walked into a little shop just outside of Barcelona, and I asked them their opening hours (since they weren't posted). The worker said, *"cerramos a las 2:00 p.m. para comer y abrimos sobre las 17 o 17.30."* Translation: we close at 2:00 p.m., for lunch, and we open around 5:00 p.m. or 5.30 p.m. This phrase *"sobre las"* means "around" and gives a lot of leeway and freedom to people not to be so exact. It definitely makes an American like me think: how the hell am I supposed to organize my day around that? It's so inconvenient. That's because I want to control my schedule.

Some cultures feel that time is out of their hands and they can't control it, because too many unforeseen and unexpected things can pop up: flat tire; bus running late; a friend or family member needing help; etc. If all of those things—and a million more—could happen and cause us to be late, then why would we have to apologize? How could we possibly control time so well?

For others, it's about religion, and God is in control, not us. When I was in Morocco and would say something that is so normal and frequent to me like: "I'll see you tomorrow," the response would often be *"Inshallah!"* or "God willing." We cannot foresee the future; anything can happen, but if God wills it, we will see each other tomorrow.

→ ACT: Pace Yourself

Here's a simple activity to see how it feels to lose control of your time.

The next time you are walking down the street, stop walking at the pace you are used to and follow the pace of someone random. This may mean that you have to slow down or speed up. Walk at the same pace as that person for at least a minute.

(Don't do it in a way that makes you look like you are stalking the person, though.)

After you've done this, answer: how did it make you feel to change your pace? Did you have to walk more slowly or quickly? Why do you think you walk at the pace you normally do? What does it say about you?

I once found myself next to an elderly couple, and I challenged myself to walk at their pace, which almost made me explode with impatience.

BUSY, BUSY, BUSY

One consequence of Americans' view of time, paired with our value of productivity, is that we always seem to be busy. When I ask an American how they are doing and what's going on, I would bet big money that they will tell me **they are busy**.

It goes back to our national culture's desire to be productive, work hard, accomplish, achieve, make money, etc. As a result, in the workplace, there is a desire to always want to be available for questions from others. This ensures that THEY can be productive and not be held up. Our own work and our desire to help others mean that we are always busy, and we tell others about it to help us connect with them or commiserate together.

One way to help us understand the outcomes of this is by comparing the ideas of Time Affluent vs. Time Famished.

TIME AFFLUENCE AND TIME FAMISHED

Time affluence means feeling like you have the time you need to do the things you want. It's a feeling that directly correlates to happiness.

Time famished is the opposite—it means you don't have the time in your day, week, month, or life to get to the things you want or need to get to, which has serious consequences. Studies show that people working full time who feel time famished are as unhappy and stressed as people who are unemployed.

These studies show that this constant state of business and the feeling of being time famished are unhealthy for us, and we need more time to disconnect, to not be busy, and to have the time to do the things we want to do.[24]

This is backed up by students who tell me that, at home, they're not just busy Monday through Friday, but Saturday and Sunday are also filled with things to do; and it's not usually things they want to do, but things they feel they have to do.

When students come abroad, this all changes. One of the hardest things for students abroad to get used to is not being scheduled every minute of the day. The free time makes them feel stressed! Let me repeat that, because it's so shocking to see in writing: the free time makes them feel stressed!

The stress comes from not knowing how to fill their free time.

This is an awesome problem to have. If you come from a culture that is time famished, study abroad gives this gift of boredom back to you, because—be honest—when was the last time you felt bored?

Study abroad allows us, and sometimes forces us, to philosophize about life, our identity, who we are, and why we feel the things we feel. Normal life doesn't always allow us the time to do that. This is a gift. It stops that busy cycle. Some students tell me that they are almost never alone at home—they are either physically with someone else or connected virtually to someone else, all the time. Take advantage of that gift of "me time" abroad!

→ ACT: Time Management

If you are abroad and don't know what to do with your free time, here are some top tips of activities that will help you to engage in the culture, not waste your time, and make the most of your study abroad investment:

---

24 Ashley Whillans, "Time Poor and Unhappy, We're Completely Strapped for Time Because We Don't Know How to Value it. Here's How to Break out of that Mindset," *Harvard Business Review,* January, 2019, www.awhillans. com/uploads/1/2/3/5/123580974/whillans_03.19.19.pdf.

- Do nothing. That's right, do nothing. Or at least nothing specific. Go for a walk. With no objective in mind, no rush, just go for a walk. When was the last time you just went for a walk?

- Create your own bucket list. Research all of the things you want to do in your city, country, and continent while abroad. Break it down by categories, or parts of town, if that helps.

- Start adding those bucket-list items to a calendar, so you have an approximate date for them. (Then, if something out of your control happens and changes it, be flexible.)

- Add the activities in this book to that calendar and that bucket list. Sign up for a newsletter with activities happening that week or month in your city. This could come from the tourist office or a private company's website like Time Out.

- Do nothing. Yep, it's back. Get used to not being scheduled every minute of the day and every day of the week.

- Don't stress if you don't get to everything on your bucket list. Have it as a guide but not a mandate.

This is an exercise in time management. You'll want to find that balance of making the most of your time, with the understanding that "making the most of your time" could mean time alone to reflect, "doing nothing."

The whole field of Time Management is incredibly important, in the US, as indicated by the thousands of books and articles written on it, showing how much we want to control time. The problem is that it's hard for people to find time to read those books in their busy schedules.

MONOCHRONIC VS. POLYCHRONIC

Monochronic cultures, like the US, take a view of time as money, place value on planning ahead, and attempt to control time, whereas polychronic cultures tend to handle more than one relationship at a time, value spontaneity, see time as more fluid and elastic, don't feel that they can control time, and know that schedules are going to change frequently.

Think of monochronic vs. polychronic this way: do you have a watch that shows the date, day, hour, minute, and seconds; arrive everywhere early; have a full calendar; and get upset when someone cancels last minute (monochronic)? Or do you not even wear a watch, rarely look at the time, have a loose schedule of activities, and arrive late to meetings; and do you, yourself, cancel last minute, often, without worrying about apologizing (polychronic)?

A REAL-LIFE EXAMPLE

*My time is my time. This is my turn. I've **earned** this time.* Those were the thoughts going through my mind when I had just waited fifteen minutes in line for my turn at a phone store and finally got up to the counter, when another customer entered the store, walked straight up to the counter, and said, "I just have a quick question—do you sell a charger for this phone?" and he holds up his phone. In the US, I would have expected the worker to say, "Excuse me, sir, but the line is back there, and this man has been waiting, and now it's his turn." But...no. The clerk said, "Let me see. Yes, we sell that; they're in the back," and he proceeded to walk him halfway back before returning to me with no apology.

What the heck was going on here?!

→ ACT: Turn the "What the Heck?!" into an "I Wonder Why...?"
Here is a trick I recommend to help us adapt to these "cultural incidents." Change the angry question and exclamation ?! to a question starting with "I wonder why..."

What I mean by that is, instead of me angrily saying/screaming to myself, *Why the heck would he interrupt my time to help someone else?!*, I remove the anger and change it to an inquisitive: *I wonder why he would interrupt my time to help someone else.*

This helps by giving us a clear mind, not fogged up by aggravation, and we learn something about ourselves and the other culture.

When I break down my original thought, I see that I'm talking about "my time," but why do I think it's "my time"? Because I look at my values and see that I consider time as money and time that I've earned by waiting in line. The other perspective might be that this store clerk can quickly and easily help someone else out and that time is not so controlled. It's easier to think that this is not universally right or wrong; it's just different. It's what's right in that particular cultural context.

The store clerk in this example was coming at the situation with a polychronic mindset whereas I was coming at it with a monochronic one—and thus the cultural clash. Guess who has to do the adapting? Me.

Now when I go into a store and see a long line, but I have a quick question, I fight my monochronic American urges to wait patiently and burst forward with: *"Una pregunta rápida…"* Quick question. And guess what? No one seems to get upset.

I just have to remember not to do that back in the US, or I'd risk some major backlash.

WAITING IN LINE

We can see that different views of time even affect how people wait in line! Here's another example:

I wish I had taken a picture of this scene, but I didn't. Luckily, it's etched in my mind. I took a group of eight students to a café to get them some coffee. It was a train-station café with a long bar where you had to go up to order. I sent them in, while I ran back to the office, for about five minutes, to grab something. When I got back, I saw that my eight students were lined up, one behind the other, at the cash register, waiting to get served—but no one had been, even after five minutes.

Half a dozen locals were spread out along the bar, ordering their coffees and breakfasts, although they had arrived after my students. When I got there, my students were all fuming that these other people were "cutting in front of them." What they hadn't realized, yet, was that in this bar, and many places in Spain, you don't wait one behind the other, you just go up to the bar and order, or you ask who is the last in line.

This flexibility in waiting in line versus a strict system of queuing up—like in the UK or the US—might not just mean you wait for your coffee, but also most likely means frustration.

By iceberging a "more chaotic" queuing method ("chaotic" from an American lens), we see that other cultures value flexibility and spontaneity over the systematic, one-at-a-time approach. And it goes back to the structure and planning of our days and control of time: if we feel we can structure, plan, and control, we can organize our time, just as if we understand the queuing system, we can feel relaxed because we know when it's our turn; it's not left up to a loose, "more-or-less" time.

FINAL WORD: ADAPTING TO TIME CULTURAL DIFFERENCES

I'm not talking about adapting to time zones, which is hard enough—they say that it takes one day for every hour of difference to adapt to time zones. From experience, I can confidently say it takes MUCH longer to adapt to cultural time differences.

After living abroad for almost twenty years, I have certainly changed my views of time. I'm more lax about punctuality and scheduling; when someone cancels a meeting, a few hours before it starts, I don't get angry like I used to; and I don't mind when people show up (a little) late or can't confirm plans with too much detail. When I can iceberg the reasons behind their decisions, I no longer judge them as rude, callous, and insensitive; instead, I understand the why behind their actions and can accept them more easily. This does not mean that I agree with what they have done or prefer it that way, though.

When you learn to shut off your Cultural Autopilot and smoothly adapt to different views of time, you will see that this helps you adapt to unpredictable situations, in general, which helps you lead a life with less anxiety, more fun, and "better use of your time"—in whatever way that means to you.

DIVE DEEPER INTO...
→ Time affluence:

"Time Affluence: The Science of Well-Being," Coursera, The University of Yale, accessed January 15, 2022, https://www.coursera.org/lecture/the-science-of-well-being/time-affluence-I6MEY.

Laurie Santos, "Episode 5: For Whom the Alarm Clock Tolls," *The Happiness Lab*, May 2020, www.happinesslab.fm/season-2-episodes/episode-5-for-whom-the-alarm-clock-tolls.

→ The cultural dimensions of time:

Edward T. Hall, *The Dance of Life: The Other Dimension of Time* (New York: Anchor 1989).

Chapter 16

SET YOURSELF APART AND LAND YOUR DREAM JOB

FUTURE YOU IN A JOB INTERVIEW

Here's the scene: two recent grads have both made it to the interview process for their dream jobs in Marketing, thanks to having study abroad on their résumés. One of them didn't have this book and ended up just skimming across the surface, during his time abroad, and the other followed the suggestions in this book and is ready to describe her experiences and growth. Here's how it plays out:

Scene 1:

Interviewer: Hello, John, I see that you studied abroad for a semester. How was it? How do you think that experience would help you in this job?

John: It was awesome! I can't explain how great it was. I learned so much and did so many cool things. I traveled, met people from all over the world, learned about the culture—like the siesta jajaja. It was really unbelievable.

How would that experience help me in this job? Hmmm. Good question. I guess I learned a lot in my classes. I took International Marketing at the local university, so…yeah, we learned a ton about the different ways people market in different countries. And all of my travels too. We traveled, like every weekend, to a new country; it was really cool to have Europe at my fingertips.

Scene 2:

Interviewer: Hello Katie, I see that you studied abroad for a semester. How was it? How do you think that experience would help you in this job?

Katie: Yeah, thanks for asking; I look for any opportunity to talk about it! It was truly an amazing experience—in a word, I would say "transformative." I feel like I grew more as a person, in four months, than I had in four years at college. It was such an intense semester, filled with challenges, struggles, and mistakes—lots of mistakes. The mistakes helped me learn so many new things, like how to maintain a sense of humor in a stressful situation, and taught me not to be afraid to take risks. For example, I took an International Marketing class at the local university, and even though my Spanish was only okay at the time, I got the courage up to ask this local Spanish student if she wanted to study together. Before going abroad, I NEVER would have had the confidence to do that. We ended up becoming great friends, she had me over to meet her family, and I ended up eating the all-important Sunday lunches with them—all in Spanish! She and I did our final project together, which was to create a Marketing plan for a small Spanish startup to break into the US market. I can see a lot of parallels, actually, between that company case study and your organization.

Which of these students would you hire?

If you are picturing yourself in this situation and thinking, uh oh, I don't know exactly how I would answer that question, you know that you have grown and learned so much, but you're not sure how to articulate it. Don't fret. That's what this chapter is for! I'll take you through how to put study abroad on your résumé, how to incorporate it into your cover letter, how to nail the job interview, and how to network.

WHAT EMPLOYERS ARE LOOKING FOR: THE CULTURAL SUPERPOWERS REVISITED

Now that we are putting it all together, let's review the Top Ten Cultural Superpowers we saw in Chapter 5.

1. **Adaptability**

2. **Empathy**

3. **Resilience**

4. **Perseverance**

5. **Sense of humor**

6. **Self-awareness**

7. **Communication**

8. **Curiosity**

9. **Confidence**

10. **Optimism**

➔》 FAST TRACK ACT: CULTURAL SUPERPOWERS BORN AND BOOSTED

Here is a fantastic activity to self-assess some of the core competencies that you have gained (born) or strengthened (boosted) abroad. I've expanded from the "Core 10" to give you a wider range of skills to recognize in yourself.

Step 1: Using the chart below, write the letter **B** to mark where you were **BEFORE** study abroad and an **N** where you feel like you are **NOW**, after study abroad.

Coaching Notes: Don't cheat yourself on this. This is just for you, so don't lie to yourself. If there was an area where you didn't grow as much as you had hoped, (1) don't beat yourself up over it; focus on the positives where you did grow. And (2) see those areas where you didn't grow much, or even went backward, as areas for improvement (which will help you answer another typical interview question).

I adapted this activity from one called Skills Acquired and Strengthened. I cannot find the original source, but I am so grateful to whoever created it, because it is extremely useful.

Example:

Resilience. Ability to bounce back from difficult challenges	1	2	3	4	5 B	6	7	8	9 N	10

I. ADAPTABILITY

Accepting of change even when the outcome is unpredictable	1	2	3	4	5	6	7	8	9	10
Ability to gain new knowledge from different experiences	1	2	3	4	5	6	7	8	9	10
Curiosity to learn more about what I don't know or don't understand yet	1	2	3	4	5	6	7	8	9	10
Ability to see things from others' perspectives and show empathy	1	2	3	4	5	6	7	8	9	10

II. CULTURAL AWARENESS

Awareness of my own values and beliefs	1	2	3	4	5	6	7	8	9	10
Awareness of my own nation's cultural tendencies	1	2	3	4	5	6	7	8	9	10
Ability to observe cultural differences and similarities	1	2	3	4	5	6	7	8	9	10
Ability to understand the why behind other cultures' behaviors and respect that even if I don't agree	1	2	3	4	5	6	7	8	9	10

III. RESILIENCE AND PROBLEM SOLVING

Self-sufficiency	1	2	3	4	5	6	7	8	9	10
Confidence in my ability to handle difficult circumstances	1	2	3	4	5	6	7	8	9	10
Ability to see other points of view as ways to solve problems vs. just using my own	1	2	3	4	5	6	7	8	9	10
Willingness to take risks	1	2	3	4	5	6	7	8	9	10

IV. COMMUNICATION AND LANGUAGE

Ability to express myself in another language other than my native tongue	1	2	3	4	5	6	7	8	9	10
Capacity to understand nonverbal communication in other cultures	1	2	3	4	5	6	7	8	9	10
Awareness of my own communication styles and how they affect communication	1	2	3	4	5	6	7	8	9	10
Superior active-listening skills	1	2	3	4	5	6	7	8	9	10

V. MINDSET

Power to see my own failures as learning opportunities, not labels	1	2	3	4	5	6	7	8	9	10
Ability to see the positive in every situation	1	2	3	4	5	6	7	8	9	10
Humility. Openness to new ideas	1	2	3	4	5	6	7	8	9	10
Maintain a sense of humor even in difficult situations	1	2	3	4	5	6	7	8	9	10

VI. RELATIONSHIP-BUILDING

Ability to successfully interact with people who hold different values and beliefs	1	2	3	4	5	6	7	8	9	10
Ability to influence peers based on their values and beliefs	1	2	3	4	5	6	7	8	9	10
Ability to suspend judgment and not discriminate	1	2	3	4	5	6	7	8	9	10
Ability to work closely with people who hold different beliefs	1	2	3	4	5	6	7	8	9	10

Step 2: Choose two areas where you have grown the most and which you feel are most important to your next interview. When you find them, write these two important words next to them: "For example..." Those are the words that will lead you into your story.

Telling a story about your new cultural superpowers is infinitely more powerful than simply stating that you grew, so take time to get this right. Luckily, if you've been doing the activities in this book all along, you should have a treasure trove of stories ready to go.

Next, write a short story that illustrates how you grew in that certain area. Make sure the story is positive and flattering to you in all ways. It's typically not a good idea to start a story about overcoming challenges by saying: "I had skipped most of my classes, and it was all coming down to the final..." or "We went out, and I was so drunk that I lost all of my friends in an area of town I wasn't familiar with..." I'm not joking when I tell you I've had students do mock interviews like that.

A better example would be, "I really didn't get along with my Czech roommates at first. Our values and ways of communicating were so different. But as I learned more about them and their cultural norms, I was able to adapt and really enjoyed having a new perspective. Now we are great friends, and they are coming to visit me in the US."

I only had you write out two of your personal anecdotes, for now, because I want to make sure you get started on it; but the more you write out while it's fresh in your head, the more prepared you will feel when the interview comes around. Your future self will thank your current self for putting in the work now.

So the next time you are in an interview for your dream job and the interviewer asks: "Tell me about a challenging time and what you did to overcome it?" you will smile, relax, and feel more prepared than ever to nail the answer.

But before you get invited to the interview, you need to wow them with your résumé and cover letter.

PUTTING STUDY ABROAD ON YOUR RÉSUMÉ

A solid résumé will put your candidacy at the top of the list, so they say, "I want to know more about this person and how they can help support my company's goals." That last part, about the company's goals, is really important to remember in this whole process: no one will give you a job to help YOU; they only hire people who will help THEM. They are not a charity. Well, maybe you will work for a charity, but the charity is to help other people, not you.

Always keep that in mind—you are trying to help them reach their goals. Then tailor your résumé, cover letter, and interview answers towards it, and you will be successful if you can prove that you are the right candidate.

Think of the résumé as an outline that starts to tell the story of why you are the best person for the job. Then the cover letter is the summary, and the interview is the full narrative.

Everyone's examples will be different, but after study abroad, you will be able to confidently say things like, "Here's why I will be a better employee because I studied abroad: I know how to deal with discomfort and fix problems that I haven't prepared for. I won't fall apart when things don't go as planned, because I am adaptive, have a tolerance for ambiguity, etc."

→ Where to Add Study Abroad Experience on Your Résumé

You could just put it under "Education," but you want to make sure it sticks out, so you could consider these sections:

- Study Abroad
- Internship Abroad
- International Education
- International Experience

You can even tailor the name of this section to the job you are going for. Let's say you want to work for a study abroad organization or a university's study abroad program—then calling it "Study Abroad" sounds perfect.

If you want to go to grad school in something international, you could say "International Education."

If you are going for a job overseas or a job that works with many overseas partners, then "International Experience" works well.

Under those sections, you want to add two to four bullet points that highlight what you think should stick out.

Those bullet points could come straight from the Cultural Superpowers Born and Boosted. For example:

Study abroad in Paris:

- Gained confidence in handling unpredictable and unfamiliar situations

- Increased fluency in French language and culture

- Boosted my willingness and confidence to take calculated risks

Depending on what you are applying for, you could also highlight some courses that you studied like:

- Cross-Cultural Psychology: A Comparative Approach

- Entrepreneurship from a European Perspective

- The African Diaspora: The Case of Immigration in Europe

→ Expand Your Story in the Cover Letter

Your cover letter allows you to give some teasers spanning three or four paragraphs to flesh out some of the skills you have acquired and strengthened and tell more of your story.

Your words should give a taste of the challenges you experienced, how you managed them with grace, in stride, and with a sense of humor, and that you learned from them. Companies are looking for employees who can weather adversity, learn, and keep moving forward, looking for new challenges. If you have followed the activities in this book, you should confidently be able to show how you accomplished all of that.

An example of a paragraph in your cover letter could be:

Through my study abroad experience in [X] country, I gained an appreciation for different perspectives, not just the one that I had cultivated from living in the United States. By interacting with my homestay family, classes with local students, and my language exchange partners, my point of view was challenged like never before. I learned to defend what I thought was right while appreciating completely different viewpoints and often adapting my sense of right and wrong.

That is just one example, but you could take any of the superpowers and expand on them in this section of your cover letter.

Now that you've piqued the interest of your future employer, through your résumé and cover letter, it's time to nail the interview.

NAILING YOUR NEXT INTERVIEW

Here are some common interview questions:

1.   What are your strengths and weaknesses?

2.   Tell me about a challenge you've overcome.

3.   Tell me about an achievement you are really proud of.

4.   Where do you see yourself in five years?

5.   Tell me about a time you've been stressed and how you dealt with it.

I hope you get a smile on your face and a sense of calm just by reading those. You are so ready for those questions! They were made for you and the chance to talk about your study abroad experience. But wait! You'll only be ready if you've prepared and rehearsed.

→ ACT: Mock Interview

Stop now and picture yourself in an interview for a job, an internship, or grad school and answer that same question that John and Katie answered at the beginning of this chapter for yourself:

I see that you studied abroad in X country for X length of time. How was it? How do you think that experience would help you in this job?

In the interview, you're going to have to articulate why you are the best person for the job—and not just articulate it but also prove it.

Let's break down what Katie did, and what John didn't do, at the opening of this chapter.

Katie talked about the core competencies that she gained or strengthened while abroad. She listed some of them, but not only that—and this is key—she gave an example to illustrate how she had grown in those areas. I have interviewed dozens, if not hundreds of candidates for positions, over the years, and there is one thing that the best interviewees do to set themselves apart: **they tell stories to illustrate their points**.

Obviously, hard skills are important, too. By hard skills, we mean the actual work that will be done. If you are going for a job as a nurse, and you don't know the difference between a broken femur and a broken tibia—or as an architect, and you've never taken an architecture course—you won't get the job just because you are highly adaptable and willing to take risks.

However, if you are on par with other candidates in terms of grades, hard skills, and experience in previous jobs, but you demonstrate that you possess the cultural superpowers we've worked on throughout this whole process, then YOU will be the one with the edge.

It's just a matter of articulating your strengths.

It's worthwhile, in a book about culture, to pause and recognize that we are supposed to talk ourselves up in a job interview for an American company—toot our own horns. This is what is expected, rewarded, and reinforced in the US.

As with almost everything we are talking about in this book, that is not universal, and bragging about your accomplishments is not "normal" in other cultures.

In fact, *Jantelagen* is a Swedish word for not thinking or talking about how you are better than anyone else. It's a cultural code that, for example, prevents Swedes from talking about how much money they earn. In the US, we cheer on people who earn a lot of money, and friends may even proudly tell you how much they have just earned, with a new job, or happily show off new cars or a nice big home. Social media is filled with people proud of the first house they just bought or a big, shiny new engagement ring.

So, if you are looking for a job in the US, and not in Sweden, then you'll have to learn to talk up your accomplishments and growth.

Feel free to take the phrases in the "Cultural Superpowers Born and Boosted" and lift them off these pages; put them on your résumé, cover letter, or in your mouth for the interview! I won't consider it plagiarism. I want you to have the best chance of talking about this experience to help you get a job. Of course, don't lie! If you don't possess those superpowers, an employer will see your lies a mile away.

CRUSHING IT AT NETWORKING, WHETHER YOU LIKE IT OR NOT

Networking is an invaluable skill to have when searching for a job. As the common phrase goes: "It's not what you know; it's who you know." Obviously, what you know is important—that's the reason for this chapter—but you never know when someone you meet will be the contact that helps you get a job.

Let me give you a tip that will serve you more than any other networking tip: when you are networking, **it's about the value you provide to the other person** as much as, or more than, what they can do for you.

I have spent hundreds of hours at networking events. I actually love them. But you can tell when someone is just looking to get something from you without reciprocating, and it's a turnoff. On the flip side, I can't tell you how many times I've recommended a good book, podcast, or restaurant to someone and they've remembered that "value," that "help," and later come back to help me out in some way.

So, in networking: think about how you can help the other person, not the other way around.

→ In-Person Networking: Tell Me about Yourself

In a networking situation, you'll get this request, which is an awesome opportunity to show off who you are, what you've done, and what sets you apart: "So tell me about yourself."

This is a tricky question because finding the line between not bragging *too* much, not boring people, and getting out the most interesting facts, in the twenty to thirty seconds you have, is not easy.

If someone asks you this, the goal is to get the other person interested enough to want to hear more. Like a job interview, a résumé, or a cover letter, you want to tailor this to the audience.

→ ACT: Tell Me about Yourself—Your Personal Elevator Pitch

Pause for thirty seconds and try to answer this question now. Say it out loud to yourself if you can, or at least say it in your head. Imagine you are at a conference, in whatever field you hope to go into, or a job fair, and you get asked this question.

You have about fifteen to thirty seconds to make an impression. As we've mentioned, your study abroad experience is a high-impact practice and should provide a wealth of great information to talk about, so now the trick is to condense it into the short period it takes you to get from the ground floor to the fifth floor. (This is where the term elevator pitch comes from)

How did that go? Did you hit the right highlights? Do you think the other person is interested in learning more about you now?

You might not be happy with your answer after one try. Don't worry! Keep practicing. It seems strange to practice such a simple question, but it's not easy to get it just right.

Hint: after you've answered this question, don't forget to ask it back to the other person! As I said above, if you're only thinking about what you can gain from them, you won't be successful. Take a genuine interest in their answer. It also works for you on a networking level because once you know more about that person, you can tailor your next questions, or the value you are adding to them, to what they've just told you. Your active-listening skills should be pretty solid by now. Write down at least one thing they've said, and follow up with them later, specifically citing something you've talked about to take your networking to the next level.

→ Online Networking

There are a million articles written about creating and boosting your LinkedIn profile, so I won't go into that here (but see the *Dive Deeper Into...* section for some resources). However, I would like to highlight that LinkedIn gives you yet one more platform to talk up your study abroad experience. You could post about the classes you took or about an "aha moment," when the lightbulb turned on about something professional, personal, academic, or cultural.

You should beef up your LinkedIn profile with the skills you strengthened, the experiences you gained, the language skills improved, and anything else that the platform allows you to do.

Whatever you do, keep communicating your value. Show potential employers how valuable you could be to them. And get as many connections as possible. You never know when one of your posts will catch the eye of someone who could be the key to your dream job.

DIVE DEEPER INTO...
→ Skills acquired during study abroad:

"Developing a Globally Competitive Workforce Through Study Abroad, The Value of Study Abroad Skills in the US Job Market," NAFSA, September 2020, www.nafsa.org/sites/default/files/media/document/developing-globally-competitive-workforce.pdf.

→ Networking:

Keith Ferrazzi and Tahl Raz, *Never Eat Alone, Expanded and Updated: And Other Secrets to Success, One Relationship at a Time* (New York: Currency, 2014).

→ Beefing up your LinkedIn profile:

"20 Steps to a Better LinkedIn Profile in 2021," LinkedIn.com, February 20, 2021, www.linkedin.com/business/sales/blog/profile-best-practices /17-steps-to-a-better-linkedin-profile-in-2017.

Chapter 17

THERE'S NO PLACE LIKE "HOME"

When I got back to campus, after my semester in Madrid, I really annoyed people. Looking back, I completely understand why. I constantly talked about how great it was and compared my stories with theirs. I started every sentence with, "Well, in Madrid they do this..." "Oh, my friend that I met in Madrid..." "You took a road trip for a weekend last semester? Well, I traveled to ten cities and five countries last semester." Yeah, I was annoying.

But I'm not alone. I hear from students all the time once they're home that the same thing happens to them.

Part of the "problem" is that we just have so many great stories to tell. But the other part of the problem is that reverse culture shock is a very real thing. Reverse culture shock is especially hard because we are not expecting it to be difficult to come "home" to our own culture.

Don't get me wrong—for most students, it is still wonderful to get back to driving your car, seeing your friends, cuddling your dog, eating your favorite foods, and enjoying some of the creature comforts you rely on back home.

However, one thing has changed since you've been away—YOU.

I put "home" in quotation marks for two reasons: there comes a time when we are not sure what home is anymore. Students travel on the weekends from their study abroad city and then get back to their study abroad housing, catching themselves saying: "it's nice to be home".

The other reason is that "home" (back in your original country) doesn't always feel like home anymore when you get back. We think of home as familiar, comfortable, and predictable, but that is not always the case when returning from study abroad, for reasons I'm about to explain.

→ ACT: The Challenges of Returning Home

Finish these sentences:

1. I expect the three most difficult things about returning home will be...

2. I am saddest about leaving behind this aspect of the culture of my
    study abroad country...

3. The biggest change I have seen in myself is...

Reflecting on these three aspects will help prepare you for the challenges of returning home and also boost your confidence by reminding you how much you've grown.

RETURNING HOME: CHALLENGES AND SOLUTIONS

I have listed, below, many of the common challenges students have, when they return home, and some potential solutions for you to overcome them.

→ Finding Faults with Your Home Country

You have changed by being abroad. Remember: "We don't see things as they are; we see them as we are." You've grown, your perspectives may have changed, and you're more adaptable, more confident, wiser, more global. What you used to perceive as right, wrong, cool, obvious, polite, or rude may have shifted.

Here's an example: maybe you came from a household where you took showers for as long as you wanted, always used paper plates and cups, and didn't think twice about the electricity you used or the consumption habits you had. Then you study abroad in a country that is much more energy conscious—you took a class on sustainability; your homestay explained to you that taking shorter showers saves water, which is a limited resource, and that using only disposable items and not recycling is bad for the environment; and you were proud of walking or taking public transportation because of the CO_2 saved. Imagine the shock when you get back to the US and see your family doing it the "normal" way (for them), which you now feel is more wasteful because you see it through a new lens. That could lead to this reverse culture shock and new debates and arguments, with friends and family, that you didn't have before. "Home" doesn't exactly feel like the home it used to be.

A more impactful example comes from 2015 and the brutal attacks in Paris by the Islamic State of Iraq and the Levant (ISIL). That attack killed 130 people and injured nearly 500.[25] We had a group of students in Morocco, at the time, staying with homestay families who were all devout Muslims. A few of our students came back angry and transformed. They said the social-media feeds of their friends and family back home were filled with anti-Islam statements, yet they had just spent three days with Muslim families who were even more horrified by the attacks than they were. They were saddened that people would commit such attacks, which go completely against Islam, and upset that the world would associate Islam with those horrific acts of violence. The students then found themselves debating their friends and families back home, backed up by some firsthand knowledge.

Solution: be patient and suspend judgment. Just like you needed to suspend judgment in the new country, that's a good rule back home. Think about how your friends and family will feel if you start to criticize their/ your culture. However, don't be afraid to tactfully open up debate about issues and help others see a different side. It's just best to be conscious of how you do it.

→ Not Able to Apply the New Knowledge and Skills

Another challenge is getting home and having the sensation of being unable to apply all of the learning that took place abroad. How do you keep the experience alive of practicing a foreign language? Of overcoming the little challenges? How do you do that when everything is back in your comfort zone?

---

25 Lori Hinnant, "2015 Paris Attacks Suspect Claims Deaths of 130 People Was 'Nothing Personal,'" PBS, September 15, 2015, www.pbs.org/newshour/tag/paris-attacks.

Solution: let me be direct—if you want some new challenges, go out and find them. Take a class on something entirely new, even online. Study a new language, explore a new area, or take on a new hobby, sport, or instrument. One great thing about study abroad is that you are always learning. Try to keep that up when you get "home."

YOU CAN'T EXPLAIN IT

→ ACT: Answer the Hardest Question You'll Ever Get About Study Abroad

I've seen this scenario play out hundreds of times...

Scene: Student back on campus after having just returned from study abroad.

Student's friend: "Hey!! You're back! **HOW WAS IT?!!**"

If this were a movie, I would play that question in slow motion—"HOOOOOOWWW WAAAAAAS IIIIIIITTT?" While zooming in on your face as it slowly scrunches into a look of horror.

How do we answer that question? How do we briefly sum up the experience of a lifetime? Or does this person have two hours to listen to everything it meant to you? How do we explain it to someone who hasn't also been through it? You have countless stories of fun, growth, laughter, tears, new friends, overcoming challenges, exploring new places, and learning so much about yourself, and the answer usually comes out one of two ways:

1. "It was amazing." Done. That's it. That's all you can say without saying everything.

2. You say everything. The faucet opens, and the flood comes out, and you tell story after story, while their eyes slowly glaze over; and you are still talking while they look at their watches and walk away, but you don't realize it.

Solution: know your audience. Here's how:

From my experience, these are the audiences that will want to hear your stories:

- Your professors (But maybe think about censoring some of your stories.)

- Your study abroad office

- Students who are thinking of going abroad. This is a key audience, which many students don't think about, but remember how you felt before going abroad—you wanted to soak up all of the intel you could.

- Anyone who helped pay for you to have this experience

- Grandparents (again, censorship)

- Parents

- Other students who studied abroad in your country

- Other students who studied abroad anywhere! Your destinations may have differed, but the experiences may very well be similar. Also, you both probably have a heightened desire to learn more about other cultures now, so this is a good chance to share.

- Friends. I put friends last on the list because it's questionable whether they want to hear your stories, no matter how much you want to tell them.

It's important to remember why someone might not want to hear about your amazing experiences. Take a minute to think about who might not want to hear your stories and why not, before reading ahead.

- Students who can't afford to study abroad. It's not cool to rub in someone's face what an awesome experience you had to someone who will not be able to do the same because they can't afford it.

- People who don't understand why you would "do such a thing." Some people said to me, "Why would you ever leave the US when you have everything here?" Some people will tell you it's too dangerous or too risky, or just that your country is the best in the world, so why would you ever leave? You may want to strategically decide when to engage in that debate and when it's best to be left alone.

- They have their own stories to tell. This may come as a surprise, but they have still been living, while you were abroad, so they may have things to share with you too. Be willing to listen (even if their stories don't seem as exciting to you). Don't get a superiority complex.

Like a good marketer, you'll learn to segment your audience. Depending on your audience, you should come up with answers that last three seconds, thirty seconds, three minutes, or thirty minutes and know who would want to hear each one.

→ ACT: 20/20 Vision

If you find an audience willing to listen to your stories for six minutes and forty seconds, here is an activity for you. Here's how it works:

Find twenty photos that bring to life different aspects of your experience abroad and put them in a slideshow (or print them out) to tell the story of your experience.

The trick is that you only get twenty seconds to describe the story behind each photo.

This not only helps guide your story and gives you a time limit; it also forces you to go through the thousands of pictures you have and find only twenty of the most important.

BOREDOM

When you are abroad, everything can be exciting. Just popping out to get some ice cream might be an adventure! When I was in Milan and hunted out the best gelato place in the entire city, I had to figure out how to get there, how to wait in line, and how to count the right currency, which looked like play money to me. When I finally got my turn, I ordered fish ice cream ("peSHe") instead of peach ice cream (peS-Kah). Luckily, they didn't serve fish-flavored gelato, so I just had to deal with getting laughed at, but I still got the best ice cream in the world! The point is that, in the US, that would not have been a story. I would have been on cultural autopilot.

And that's just the excitement of getting ice cream—not even mentioning the epic travel, amazing new friends, intense conversations, "lightbulb moments," incredible places I'd never been to before, and more.

This often feels impossible to replicate back home. But it's not impossible.

HERE'S HOW TO KEEP THE EXPERIENCE ALIVE
→ ACT: You Did It! Now, What's Next? Your Home Bucket List
You did it! You made it through a successful study abroad experience with all its ups and downs. We've talked about the challenges, but these are Probletunities! There is actually so much to look forward to after returning home. Now, what's next?

→ Your Home Bucket List

When I got back from study abroad, I realized that I knew the history of St. Petersburg, Russia, Madrid, Spain, and Milan, Italy, better than I knew the history of my home city of Chicago. So I decided to change that. I had a newfound motivation to learn more of the history of my own city, and I had the tools to do it. I bought a guidebook to Chicago. I signed up for tours of the city. I started to interview people, in Chicago, about their favorite spots and things to do. It was like the Cultural Blueprint activity in Chapter 6 but for my own city! And it was fantastic. I gained a better appreciation and pride in my city, and it was even better because I was able to use new tools to go deeper.

→ Don't Stop Using Your New Language

If you improve a second language, while abroad, keep it going. Take more classes; find a language exchange, on campus or in town; do online apps; join a language club at school (or start one!); watch TV in that language; listen to podcasts; read books; or do video calls with the people you met abroad. Admittedly it won't be as easy as when you were immersed in it, but I guarantee there are more ways than you think to keep practicing.

When I got back from Spain, I volunteered to teach English to Mexican children in my town, so I was able to keep practicing my Spanish (with their parents) and got to learn about Mexican culture. You could see if your town has something similar available.

SEEK OUT PEOPLE FROM OTHER CULTURES

If you get a real buzz, like I do, from learning about other cultures, then find out how to do that now that you are back. Most university campuses have an international-student population. Go seek them out. You now know how it feels to be a fish out of water in a new culture, so maybe you could be their cultural mentor. Ask them the beautiful question, "What's new to you?" and get a cultural conversation started.

TRAVEL TO OTHER PARTS OF THE US

Take a road trip to visit a new city you've never been to. I have former students who send me photos of their reunions, going to visit each other around the US or deciding to meet in a city that's new to all of them and explore it together.

VOLUNTEER AT YOUR STUDY ABROAD OFFICE—TALK TO PROSPECTIVE STUDENTS

Remember how many questions you had, before you studied abroad, and how you wished you had someone who had been there before? You can usually volunteer at your study abroad office to talk with students who are about to go abroad; they will want to soak up all of your stories.

→ ACT: Keep the Journal Going

When you get back home, keep your journal going! Write down the things you see and experience that stick out to you. Why do they stick out to you? What's unusual that used to be usual? How are you handling that? What differences do your friends and family see in you? How does that make you feel? Can you iceberg them?

Research shows there is a connection between journaling and brain elasticity, so it helps keep the learning going. And who knows, maybe someday you will look back at your journal and write a book based on your experiences.

KEEP THE GROWTH MINDSET

Just because your study abroad has finished, it doesn't mean that the learning finishes. What else haven't you learned to do YET?

→ ACT: Areas of Improvement

Remember the Cultural Superpowers Born and Boosted? In the last chapter, we took the areas where you were the **strongest** and used them to help in your job search process. Now we want to look at where you are the **weakest** so you can see what to work on. Find the greatest areas of improvement and think about ways to work on them in this next stage. Create a plan of action for improvement.

→ ACT: Your Identity Revisited—Iceberg Yourself Again

Waaaay back in Chapter 2, you iceberged yourself. If you had to do that again, now, how would it look different, and what does that mean now that you are home?

We discover so much about ourselves, while we are abroad, that I dedicated an entire chapter to it in this book (Chapter 4). Now that you're home, it's a good time to reflect on it again.

1. Would anybody see that any of your behaviors have changed now that you're home? (This is what is explicit above the water.)

2. Write down whether you had any positive or negative experiences related to your different identities while abroad.

3. How has study abroad changed your values and/or identity? (This is what might be invisible below the water.)

4. What values, beliefs, and behaviors did you learn, in the host country, that you hope/plan to maintain now that you're back in the US?

5. How might these values, beliefs, and behaviors conflict with US culture?

For example, we hear from some BIPOC students that they had more positive experiences abroad, related to race, relative to their experiences in the US. Students from certain parts of the US may experience less racism abroad than back in their home city.

The same could be said for LGBTQ students who come from an area of the US where they don't feel comfortable being open about their sexuality, but abroad lived in a city—like Barcelona, for example—where you see gay couples together all the time, a huge Gay-Pride festival filled with people and families from all over, and an openness that could make them feel comfortable abroad, only to be shocked again when returning home.

YOUR WELL-BEING BACK HOME

I dedicated an entire chapter to your well-being while abroad, but your well-being upon return is important and could be taxed and challenged, in ways that you were not expecting. Find out what might stress you out. Do you feel more prepared to handle those stressors now that you have the experience of adapting to other cultures? If you are struggling, remember the basics: get sleep and get exercise. Next, go back to that list of people who want to hear your stories, and talk to them. Reminiscing often helps us feel better. Think about the new and exciting challenges and opportunities now that you are home. Write out your SMART goals, again, now that you are back; plan things that you can look forward to; and keep yourself busy with things you love to do. And, of course, if you are really struggling, go and see someone professional for help.

DIVE DEEPER INTO...

→ Reentry culture shock:

Your study abroad office! Ask your study abroad offices for resources, and I imagine they will have plenty to share.

→ Go back abroad:

Find all kinds of resources on www.GoAbroad.com.

IT DOESN'T END HERE

The growth you've experienced, during study abroad, doesn't end now that the program is over. Just look at what these students said one month, four years, ten years, and twenty-five years after studying abroad: Testimonial from a student **one month** after returning home:

"My study abroad experience helped me increase my self-confidence, increase my independence, and develop my interpersonal communication skills. It encouraged me to break out of my comfort zone more often, expanded my curiosity of the world, enhanced my ability to think critically about culture and the world, and clarified my future educational and/or career goals."
—Brenley B, Abroad Summer 2021

Testimonial from a student **four years** after returning home:
"I studied abroad almost four years ago now, and I still draw on the experience every day. There's no doubt that it helped me land my dream job at a fire agency as a firefighter. I've wanted this career since I was a child, and thanks to everything I learned during my semester abroad, it's finally become a reality."
—Perry T, Abroad 2017

Thirteen years later:

"I recently just met up with some of the people I studied abroad with, and they reminded me how I was a changed person when I came back from my intern experience in Barcelona. I knew I had grown in ways that I couldn't quite comprehend, but they saw it in me. Even though that was in 2009, I still think about the experience every day. I don't think I would be in this incredible job that I'm in now if it wasn't for my internship abroad. I'm so thankful, every day, that I took that leap of faith so many years ago."
        —Bailey B, Abroad 2009

Twenty-five plus years later:

"This book and my twenty-five years working in study abroad is my testimonial. There is no question that my first study abroad experience, a short eight weeks in St. Petersburg, Russia, changed my life. That pioneering journey, and my first time out of the United States, put me on this path to lead a full, happy, and meaningful life and led me to this job that—calling it my dream job feels like it comes up short—fulfills me in so many ways."
        —You guessed it, Rich K,
    Abroad for the first time in 1996

As you can see, study abroad can be a life-changing, transformational experience that will be with you for the rest of your years. But it doesn't just happen; you need to ACT.

This book gave you the activities that will be most useful on this incredible journey and tips on how to get the most out of your study abroad experience, so you don't waste this amazing opportunity to grow personally and professionally, truly reap the benefits of study abroad, and come out the other side feeling more confident, adaptable, resilient, and employable. Now you should be ready to take on any challenge this world throws at you. Here's how we did it.

Chapter 1: We started by looking at the useful information to know before you go abroad. We looked at your purpose, SMART goals, and ways of thinking about logistics like: should I choose to live in a homestay, an apartment, or a residence hall?

Chapter 2: We explored the all-important idea of cultural autopilot. We defined the word culture and began to understand the gigantic importance of culture, using a new verb: to iceberg. Like fish out of our normal waters, we learned to start sharpening our observation skills and dive deeper, to learn more about why people do what they do. This is an essential tool to help us adapt.

Chapter 3: One of the most important growth lessons was how we changed our mindsets to start reframing failure and problems as powerful learning opportunities.

Chapter 4: Although it seems odd at first, going abroad helps us learn as much about ourselves—our own cultures and identities—as the places that become our new homes.

Chapter 5: With lessons from Experiential Learning Theory and true anecdotes of my former students, we realized that, although this journey abroad will be challenging, there are so many benefits that make it incredibly worthwhile.

Chapter 6: We outlined practical tips and strategies to get to know your new home city.

Chapter 7: Our national cultures have an incredible impact on who we are and why we act the way we do. This chapter helped you learn more about your national culture and provided valuable activities to help you understand the national culture you are studying in.

Chapter 8: If one of your goals is to increase proficiency in a second language, here you received over twenty tips—conventional and unconventional—to help you do that while helping you immerse and adapt.

Chapter 9: We debunked the popular myth that just knowing a language is enough for you to communicate effectively. Even if you are studying abroad in a country where you already speak that language, there will be plenty to learn and plenty of room for cultural mishaps.

Chapter 10: Nonverbal communication comprises the majority of our communication. That means that a lack of understanding of nonverbal cues can cause massive confusion and make it harder to adapt. This chapter gave you a different perspective on communication and tips to help you communicate more effectively without even saying a word.

Chapter 11: Whoever thought you could grasp cultural knowledge through food? This chapter converted what every single person in the world does every day—eats—into a lens for cultural understanding.

Chapter 12: And what's food without drink? From hot drinks to cold drinks to alcohol consumption around the world, we used drinks as another prism, to understand why people drink the way they do and what that means to your experience abroad.

Chapter 13: Absorbing all of this information, and allowing yourself to grow abroad, greatly depends on your ability to stay of sound body and mind. This chapter described that importance and gave strategies to achieve it.

Chapter 14: How can close-talkers, PDA, and waiting in line have such a huge impact on your study abroad experience? What can you do when that makes you feel uncomfortable? We discovered several strategies to guide you through the differences in personal-space perspectives.

Chapter 15: This chapter gave us frameworks and examples to comprehend how different cultures view time, what that means to how we schedule our days, and why we might get upset when someone cancels a meeting, last-minute, or cuts in line.

Chapter 16: Your experience is over, and you're working on getting a job, an internship, or acceptance into grad school. This chapter showed you how to put it all together, on your résumé and cover letter, and how to nail your next job interview; and it provided top networking tips.

Chapter 17: Just when you thought going "home" would be the easy part, you're smacked in the face with reverse culture shock and difficult challenges when you return to your home country. This chapter shared strategies other students have used to get through those challenges and use them to their advantage.

WHAT DOES STUDY ABROAD TEACH US ABOUT LEADING A FULFILLING LIFE?

Doctors and nurses interviewed people in palliative (end-of-life) care—people who know they are living their last days of life due to disease—and asked them what they wish they had done differently during their lives.

When I read the five categories of their answers, I could not help but see the benefits of study abroad even more clearly:

They wish they had:

1. Led a fuller life, less fearful of, and more open to, change. They wish they had learned to bounce back from setbacks.

2. Led a more authentic life and done what they wanted to do, not what others expected of them.

3. Been more present and learned how to savor the moment they were in and take advantage of each and every day.

4. Lived with more joy and laughed more; not taken themselves so seriously. They wish they had found delightful moments in the day full of "awe."

5. Lived with more love, loved what they did for a living, said, "I love you," more, and served what they loved.

I look back at the cultural superpowers born and boosted by study abroad, and I see:

1. Adaptability to unfamiliar situations, resilience, and viewing failure as a way to learn and as something that helps you to lead a fuller life.

2. Self-awareness and confidence as a way to lead a more authentic life.

3. Curiosity, being comfortable on your own, and disconnecting as the path to learning to savor the moment.

4. Optimism, keeping a sense of humor in difficult situations, and understanding your own values as the path to live with more joy.

5. Increased empathy, improved communication skills, and getting to know people from around the world as a way to live with more love.

WHAT'S A CHAPTER WITHOUT AN ACT?
→ Here Is One Last Activity, and It's About Gratitude.

→》 FAST TRACK ACT: WRITE A LETTER OF THANKS TO ANYONE WHO HELPED MAKE THE EXPERIENCE POSSIBLE

1. That might be your parents for **financially** supporting you; it might be others who financially supported you.

2. Think about who supported you **emotionally** and write them a letter of thanks. Tell them what the experience meant to you.

3. Write a letter of thanks to anyone who supported you **logistically**— your study abroad office, your professor, your academic advisor. Thank them for helping make this experience happen.

4. Hey, if this book helped, you could **write me a letter at RichKurtzman@FishinWaterBook.com**. There will be nothing more satisfying to me than hearing from you. Feel free to ask me any other questions specific to you. I promise I will read and respond to every single one. Of course, with my growth mindset, let me know if you have constructive criticism or suggestions for the book; I would be thankful to receive that from you as well—sugarcoated or not!

5. Finally, write a **letter to yourself**, to thank yourself for taking this risk. You left everything you knew and understood behind and jumped into an experience that was:

    a. Unknown
    b. Unpredictable
    c. Uncomfortable

And you made it

    a. Known
    b. Predictable
    c. Comfortable

That is no small feat, and it deserves a huge congratulations.

At the beginning of this book, I made the bold claim that deciding to study abroad, with the right tools and the right mindset, would be the best decision of your life. I truly hope that your experience has lived up to that promise.

Do you want more?

Find bonus material at FishinWaterBook.com.

MY GRATITUDE TO YOU
→ Thank You for Making the World a Better Place

Study abroad has not just benefited you; it has benefited the world. Imagine if everyone learned to see things from the perspective of others and was not afraid of the cultures and behaviors they didn't understand, then actually made an effort to understand them. In my opinion, there would be fewer wars, hatred, division, and misinformation.

Now that you've made that transformation, what's next? How do you bring this back to your homelife and make a small impact on your world? I don't have all the answers, but I see the value in the questions, especially for someone like you who now harnesses some new cultural superpowers.

Thank **YOU** for making the world a little smaller and for putting in the hard work to help this world understand each other, a little more, no matter where we come from.

ACKNOWLEDGMENTS

Writing this book has been much more rewarding and much more work than I ever anticipated. I could not have gotten here, though, without the help of so many people who guided me, put up with me, and helped me in every way.

Kerry, my incredible wife, this book absolutely would not have happened without you. Not only have you given me nearly twenty years of joy and intercultural learning, but your support throughout this book-writing process has meant all the difference. You gave me stories and advice, read drafts, and were my sounding board. You suffered through my incessant talk about the book, and you never blinked an eye when I hid away to write, even though it meant you had to take care of two small, rambunctious kids and a maniacal puppy. I am eternally grateful for that support and for every moment we've spent together.

Jack and Emma, I love you more than you know. I love watching you grow up with the challenges and opportunities of navigating three languages and four cultures. You are amazing, brave, and both mean so much to me. Thank you for understanding that Daddy often had to say no to playing with you, so I could work on the book over the last twelve months. There's nothing I enjoy more than watching you grow up and gain your own cultural superpowers.

Mom, I would not be here, writing this book if it wasn't for you. You supported me, emotionally and financially, during my early study abroad years. I knew you were always there for me, no matter what challenge I was facing, and that kept me going. As hard as it must have been for you, you didn't let me come home from Barcelona! I know you regret that decision now that I've been here for twenty years instead of two, but that's what makes me all the more thankful. You are wonderful, supportive, and generous beyond belief.

My sister, Pauli, the pioneer. Had you not studied abroad in Russia before me, I'm not sure I would have had the confidence to do it too. Thank you for the inspiration!

Dad, thank you for all of the love and support you provide from thousands of miles away.

I want to acknowledge my professors at Illinois Wesleyan University who pushed me deeper into languages, cultural studies, and study abroad. You made me feel like I had no other choice, and in the end, you were right. I'm so honored that we are still in contact, twenty-five years later, and that I can call you amigo/as and colleagues. That's very special to me. Carolyn Nadeau, Carmela Ferradans, Marina Balina, and Mauricio Parra, you are the best.

Devika Milner, your expertise in the world of study abroad and your contributions helped shape this book, even before the first word was written. Thank you for always being willing to hear my ideas and share your own.

Bill Martens and Carla Slawson, your creative and positive energy was an enormous help for me. Some of the phrases in this book came straight from your mouths onto the page, because you say it much better than I can. I am so grateful to both of you.

Robyn Walter, thank you for your guidance, feedback, and unique perspectives, and for listening to me drone on and on about the book.

EJ Yoder and John Sunnygard, I am beyond lucky to call you friends and colleagues. I learn so much from you every time we are together.

Thank you for taking the time to read some early drafts of these chapters and provide non-sugar-coated advice.

Brenley Bruxvoort, your feedback from a student perspective was priceless! I can't thank you enough.

Thank you to all of the study abroad alumni and current students who have allowed me to quote them: Brianna Fogo, Bryan Kim, Perry Taylor, Bailey (Bintz) O'Leske, Nadia Judge, Scott Rich. May your words go on to inspire those who come after you!

I am so grateful to the wonderful people at Scribe Media for guiding me through this process of getting a book out into the world, and especially to Emily Gindlesparger and Chas Hoppe. I've told you before; you are brilliant! Thank you for your incredible coaching, for not just giving me the answers but helping me to come up with them. Hussein Al-Baiaty, your positive energy is contagious. Thank you to Rebecca Lown for spending so much time with me on the book cover and for the beautiful result. Thank you to Laura Cail for your masterful editing skills and Bianca Pahl for keeping it all together. And to all the other authors at Scribe whom I've gotten to know—every week I learned something from you, and I so appreciate it.

To my team at Barcelona SAE, thank you for working so hard to create the magic of study abroad for all of our students. The world is a better place because of the effort you put in. I could not ask for a better *equipo*.

Christina Thompson, thank you for providing your wisdom and resources for the section on identity. Your work in DEI is sorely needed, and your determination is so admirable.

Darcy York, thank you for sharing this expat experience with me and for your hilarious stories—several of which made it into the book.

Elena Villaescusa, your anecdotes of cultural mishaps are genius. Thank you for allowing me to share some of them with the world.

Kristin Uyl, without your stellar organizational skills, my *Culture Stock: Tips and Strategies for Increasing Cultural Awareness* newsletter would probably just be sitting on my computer instead of in front of thousands. Thank you!

Troy Peden, thank you for helping me see the world and for creating the volunteer program in the Philippines that opened my eyes to a different, wonderful place. Your perseverance and hard work encourage me to always see the possibilities despite the obstacles.

To all of you who provided stories and anecdotes that I've used in the book. You've remained anonymous in these pages, but you know who you are. Thank you for taking risks, getting out of your comfort zones, and making mistakes so we can laugh with you together.

To all of the study abroad companies that I've had the privilege to work with and learn from in the past: CIS Abroad, CIS Australia, IES Abroad, CEA, Morocco Exchange, and World Learning. I've gained knowledge from all of you that has shaped my career and the activities in these pages.

Professor BVP, although my master's degree with you was Spanish Applied Linguistics, as my advisor and professor, you taught me so much more. You taught me how to be a teacher and how students learn, and you inspire me still to this day with everything that you've done and continue to do.

I am grateful to my former boss in Barcelona, Josep Miró, for giving me the best advice: "Rich, you have to adapt to the culture; the culture is not going to adapt to you," and teaching me cultural lessons that have served me well over the years.

Thank you to all of the cultural gurus in the field who have provided theories, research, and activities that I have used, over and over, to help thousands of students expand their horizons and learn to see the world from a different perspective.

I am grateful to everyone who works in the field of International Education and works day in and day out to allow students to have this life-changing experience.

And last, but certainly not least, thank you to my international gang of friends in Barcelona. You are my family. All of those times you made fun of me for being "so American" have been put to good use.